Cooking

with

Herbs

and spices

Marcia Neely

Prairie Projects Press

Photographs by John Neely
Artwork by Doug Pederson

Prairie Projects Press
155 60th St. NW, Benson, MN 56215

ISBN 978-1-4276-4046-8

Designed and printed in the United States of America

For the Milan Village Arts School in Milan, MN, and the
students of my Cooking with Herbs class, which
inspired the development of this book

Dedicated to the memory of my mom, Mae Pederson Stoen, whose culinary
skills and love for cooking and baking inspired my own

With special thanks to my sister, Susan Schei, whose attraction to the
wilderness, native plants, and wild creatures stimulated my interest;
for my husband, John, whose love and able assistance with photography
and computer skills made this publication possible;
for my brother, Doug Pederson, whose artistic genius amazes
me and whose values help ground me;
for my friends, Don and Helen Berheim, whose friendship nurtures me;
and for my long-time friend, Nancy Overcott, a writer and
naturalist and the editor of this publication

Table of Contents

History and philosophy of culinary herbs i

Use of herbs in cooking iii

Preserving herbs v

Descriptions of culinary herbs and spices ix

Suggestions regarding recipe ingredients xxix

Breads 1

Meat & fish 9

    Beef 10

    Chicken 15

    Pork 33

    Fish 40

Pasta & rice 43

Salads 53

    Salad dressings 70

Soups 75

Vegetables 87

Miscellaneous, including appetizers 97

~~~~~

ℋistory and philosophy of culinary herbs

𝒞ulinary herbs likely began their debut in cooking as preservatives. Long, long before canning and refrigeration became the primary methods of preserving food, our ancient ancestors, predominantly women, discovered that many plants had qualities that prevented or delayed putrefaction and spoilage.

Perhaps by watching animals use the herbs, our ancestors also recognized some plants' value in treating or preventing disease. Modern science has discovered antibacterial, antifungal, and antiviral attributes in almost all of the herbs we use in cooking, herbs like rosemary, thyme, garlic, and sage. Scientists also recognize the antispasmodic effect of some of the culinary herbs, especially those in the mint family, and thus their aid to digestion. Other culinary herbs and spices assist digestion by stimulating the flow of gastric juices.

Using herbs in the preparation of foods to keep meat from spoiling and to diminish the molding of grain products likely led to the development of a taste for these plants. This led to cherishing the fragrant aroma and the pungent taste of basil, sage, and flat-leaved parsley, the piquant heat of lemongrass, hot peppers, and garlic, and the sweet spiciness of coriander, cinnamon, cloves, and nutmeg.

All of these herbs and spices added essential vitamins and minerals and other micro-nutrients to the diet that today we recognize as life enhancing and disease preventing.

The diet of our ancestors was much more varied in nutrients than our modern diets. Our forebears recognized or intuited that good health depended upon eating a wide range of foodstuffs with a variety of nutrients, including those that come from herbs.

As cultures flourished, so did their cuisines. Herbs became one of the primary influences in distinguishing one culture's food from another's. The Europeans developed cooking methods that used primarily the leafy parts of such herbs as basil, sage, thyme, oregano, tarragon, and parsley. In the Americas, particularly in the warmer climates, hot peppers, cilantro, and allspice became fundamental parts of the cooking pattern.

The Middle and Far East developed the spices because their climates allowed for the lush growth of the cinnamon, nutmeg, and clove trees. Spice and herb trade was the foundation of much of the ancient economy.

Spices, technically, are those tasty elements of a plant that are harvested from the bark, seeds, or sometimes flower buds, while herbs are the leafy parts of plants that contain healthy or tasty elements. The words "herb" and "spice" are sometimes used interchangeably, and habit has designated some savory plant parts as herbs, although they may technically be spices, and vice versa. Yet, most commonly "culinary herb" refers to the leafy parts, such as rosemary and thyme sprigs, that are used for health or taste, while "spice" is reserved for that which comes from the bark, such as cinnamon, or is the seed, such as nutmeg, or the flower bud, such as cloves.

The recipes that follow, which are my creations, generally do not distinguish between herb and spice. Concentration is on the use of herbs that will grow in the northern latitudes where I live. Apart from my mom's recipe for cardamom bread, the recipes were never intentionally copied from other sources, although many are based on foods I've eaten or recipes I've used. Since countless varieties of recipes exist, I apologize for the inclusion of any recipe that appears to be a duplication of someone else's creation.

Marcia Neely

~~~~~

$\mathcal{U}$se of herbs in cooking

$\mathcal{T}$raditional U.S. Midwestern diet, especially that influenced by Scandinavian culture, made limited use of herbs. Now, influenced by cuisines from around the world, herbs have become essential ingredients of both restaurant fare and home cooking.

There are few rules for using herbs in cooking, the primary one being simply to use those that taste good to you. Experiment with a variety of herbs. Go to farmers markets and talk with the herb growers to discover their ideas and secrets. Grow some of your own.

Some herbs lend themselves better to one dish than another. Tarragon is especially good with chicken and fish, for instance. The Mediterranean herbs such as basil, rosemary, thyme, and parsley are particularly appealing in pasta dishes and go well with tomatoes. Sage and thyme are traditionally used with poultry. Bay leaves season soups and stews, as well as many other dishes. Mexican fare does well with hot peppers, epazote, cilantro, and influenced by the cuisines of Spain and France, often includes garlic, basil, mustard, mint, parsley, lemongrass, and thyme.

 Asian cooking concentrates on the spices, such as cinnamon, coriander, and cumin and makes heavy use of ginger. Garlic adds flavor and a little heat to the cuisine of many cultures.

All the herbs and spices may be experimented with in various dishes, creating new, interesting, and sometimes wonderful flavors. Find the herbs that suit the foods you are creating.

When possible, use fresh herbs because they are generally the most aromatic and flavorful, although most that are properly dried or frozen are nearly as good, especially when used in dishes that cook long enough to allow the herbs to re-hydrate and exude their flavors.

The best flavor of spices is had by using whole spices, grinding them as you use them.

Adding herbs near the beginning of cooking allows the flavors to penetrate deeply; adding some at the end of dishes that cook for a long time generally better preserves the enzymes in the herbs and their healthful value.

The descriptions of herbs and spices starting on page ix will give you some added guidance, as well as provide information about the plants' origins and health values.

~~~~~

$\mathcal{P}$reserving herbs

$\mathcal{H}$erbs with leafy parts are preserved by freezing, drying, or keeping in vinegar. Seeds will dry without special attention if kept in an airy, not too humid, location. Depending upon the variety, garlic lasts for many months simply by leaving the bulb exposed to the air, especially in dry, cool places. Some hot peppers, including most cayenne varieties, will dry if simply left exposed to dry air; however, the larger peppers require a dehydrator or slightly warm oven.

Herbs preserved by drying are best used within a year, although they will maintain much of their flavor for many years. Vinegars, too, are best used within a year, as are herbs that are frozen. Below are descriptions of these preservation methods.

The descriptions that follow this section provide additional preservation information for specific herbs.

Drying

Drying is used predominantly for the leafy herbs such as basil, parsley, rosemary, sage, tarragon, and thyme.

The first task is to wash the plant, usually by sloshing it in cool water, then allowing it to air dry for a short time. Most herbs can simply be hung or placed on screens in a clean, dry place and allowed to dry on their own. An exception is basil which will often rot with this method.

However, the taste, color, and healthful value of an herb is better preserved with quicker drying in a dehydrator at $105-115$ degrees. Some herbs need only a few hours while others require many hours, and the humidity level will make significant difference in the drying time. Some ovens that can be turned down to very low temperatures will also work as dehydrators. A screen similar to that used in dehydrators should be used and the oven door should be left slightly ajar.

Once dried, herbs must be stored in airtight containers. With large quantities that will be stored for a time, vacuum bags are preferable to jars.

Freezing

Many culinary herbs can be snipped, rinsed, air dried, and then frozen in bags. It works well to freeze dill, sage, rosemary, thyme, and tarragon on the stem. However, you can also snip the leaves off the stem, bag, and freeze.

Chives, oregano, and parsley, are best snipped into small pieces, put into the freezer on a cookie sheet for an hour or so, and then quickly bagged. Use vacuum bags, freezer bags, or double bags, removing as much air as possible.

A method for use in stews, soups, etc. is to dice the herbs finely (or use a food processor), put into ice cube trays, top with water, and freeze. To preserve freshness, remove the cubes from the tray, place in a plastic bag, and return to the freezer.

Basil is best frozen by blending and mixing it with olive oil, then freezing it in ice cube trays, and finally bagging it. Alternatively, make pesto and freeze the pesto.

Preserving in vinegar

A fun and creative way of preserving herbs is to make herbal vinegars. The leafy parts of most herbs, as well as garlic cloves and hot peppers, can be well preserved in vinegar. For tarragon, this is the ideal method.

Using a white or red wine vinegar or apple cider vinegar, the basic method is to fill a sterile jar with the herb or herbs of choice; then fill the jar with the vinegar and allow it to rest in a dark place for about one month.

After letting the herbs steep in vinegar for a month or so, taste to ensure the flavor has well penetrated, then either allow the vinegar to steep a couple weeks longer or strain the herb from it. If you wish to make the herbal vinegar look especially attractive, add a few sprigs of any included herb, using mostly those that are smaller-leaved, to a sterilized tall jar. Then add the vinegar, cap, and, if desired, seal with wax. For more ideas and recipes, several books on making herbal vinegars are available.

~~~~~

Descriptions of culinary herbs and spices

Allspice   *Pimenta dioica*

Allspice has a flavor that suggests some combination of cinnamon, nutmeg, and cloves, but it actually comes from the dried green berries of a tree that is native to the West Indies, Mexico, and Central America. It is used extensively in breads and desserts, but also in salads, pastas, stews, sausage, and to flavor peas and carrots, as well as for barbecue, chocolate, and tomato sauces.

As with most spices, the whole berries have a greater shelf life than does ground allspice.

Not well known for medicinal properties, allspice nonetheless assists digestion and is a mild external anesthetic.

Anise   *Pimpinella anisus*

Anise for seed and star anise, which is described later in this section, come from separate plants. Anise, native to the Middle East, is the seed of the *Pimpinella* plant, an herb described in antiquity that has a licorice-like taste. The ground seed of anise is primarily used for sweets and breads, but is also used in flavoring stews, soups, fish and shellfish.

Anise seed is said to cure hiccoughs. Magical qualities, including an ability to ward off evil and increase psychic abilities, are also attributed to it.

Because it loses flavor after grinding, it is best to buy anise as whole seeds and grind them as you need them. A mortar and pestle is ideal for this purpose.

$\mathscr{B}$asil

Ocimum basilicum

Basil is a popular culinary herb, especially in pastas, marinara sauces, and other Italian dishes. The flavor of the leaves increases when cooked. Fresh leaves are good in salads, adding a special pungency, and make a great dressing when chopped and blended with vinegar and oil. Make pesto by pounding or grinding basil leaves, pine nuts or other nuts, and mixing with olive oil and Parmigiano cheese.

Genovese basil is more full flavored than sweet basil and is typically used in pasta and pesto. Today, there are also many flavored varieties, such as lemon and cinnamon basil. Experiment to discover your favorites.

Basil was known in antiquity. The Greek word for basil means royal. It is an uplifting herb that is useful for nervous exhaustion as well as for "down in the dumps" feelings, tension headaches, and insomnia. It helps neutralize past damage from drug use, especially marijuana use. In addition, basil lowers fevers, is antispasmodic, antibacterial, anti-parasitic, and improves digestion.

Basil grows well from seed, especially if planted as soon as the spring frosts are over. Although the plant can be started inside and transplanted later, it produces almost as early if planted directly in the garden. North of zone 4, however, plants work better than direct seeding. Using both green and purple-leaved varieties makes a beautiful contrast in a garden.

Harvest the leaves before flowering for cooking. Pinch back the flowers to keep the harvest going longer. Basil can be air-dried, but takes a long time and often rots before drying, so is best done in a dehydrator at a temperature of 110-115 degrees. It is never quite as flavorful dried as fresh.

$\mathscr{B}$ay leaves

Lauris nobilis

Native to Asia minor and the Mediterranean, bay is a well known aspect of cuisines of that area and, now, much of the world. The pungent aroma and slightly bitter fruity taste of the leaves has made it a staple for flavoring stews, soups, chowders, and stocks.

Bay leaves are used in their dry, not fresh, state because their flavor develops with proper drying in the sun. Generally the bay leaf is added whole near the beginning of cooking, then removed before serving because the leaves are very difficult to chew. The leaves, however, can be crushed and ground and then left in the dish.

Although not particularly noted for its medicinal value, the bay leaf was touted for its magical properties in ancient times. In the games of ancient Greece and Rome, garlands of bay leaves were used to crown victors.

Black pepper   *Piper nigrum*

Native to South India, black pepper is produced from the green not quite ripe berries of the tropical vine, *Piper nigrum*. Referenced in many ancient texts, it is now ubiquitous in the cooking of all countries since its pungent aroma and hot and woody taste adds flavor to almost all dishes.

Although pepper has limited medicinal use, it has been used for diarrhea, earache, gangrene, heart disease, and joint pain.

Occasionally you will see recipes calling for white pepper, which is made from the seed of the pepper berries with the skin and outer layer of the fruit removed.

Capers   *Capporis spinosa*

The aromatic and salty spiciness of capers is a favorite on fish and in pastas. It has been introduced to the American cuisine fairly recently, but is native to the cuisines of Sicily and Italy.

Capers are the unopened flower buds of a plant that grows in the Mediterranean area. The prepared caper is the dried, salted, and pickled bud, or sometimes the pickled fruit called caper berries.

Although the caper is naturally aromatic with a lemony flavor, its saltiness is what predominates. Salads, vegetables, pizzas, and pasta and meat sauces are among the dishes in which you will find capers.

Although some parts of the caper plant have been used medicinally, the bud is not particularly known for its medicinal attributes.

Cardamom   *Elettaria cardamomum*

Cardamom comes from the seeds that are found inside the cardamom pod. The tough pod is rarely used in cooking or baking. This spice is common in Indian and oriental cuisines, but is also used in sweet dishes and drinks and to flavor pickles and fish. My mother used cardamom to make a traditional Danish sweet bread for holidays.

Cardamom seeds are always ground before using, but nonetheless, for best flavor, it is best to buy cardamom in the pods, separate the seeds, and grind them yourself.

This spice assists digestion and diminishes flatulence. Aphrodisiac qualities are attributed to it.

Cayenne   *Capsicum annuum*

Cayenne is the red shiny fruit of an annual pepper plant variety that provides a spicy heat to any dish. Cayenne and other peppers are common in everything from hot sauces to curries, almost all Mexican and South American dishes, chilies, and many soups. A pinch or two of the dried pepper will give interest to any salad dressing and add flavor and slight heat to pastas. Mexican and South American cultures have used it in cooking and medicine for centuries.

Cayenne peppers, as well as other hot peppers, are vegetable garden plants that like full sun and a lot of heat. They are best harvested when they turn fully red. The pepper may be used fresh, usually minced, or may be dried, then pulverized into powder.

Cayenne is a stimulant for the whole body. It increases blood flow, tones the nervous system, relieves indigestion, and stimulates action. It may even ease the pain of shingles and migraines and restrict cardiac damage if used immediately after a heart attack. Although it may seem counter-intuitive, cayenne helps heal the mucosa of the stomach and intestine. It also encourages sweating and is antibacterial, so is good against infections.

Cayenne is also helpful for persons whose extremities are cold and for that purpose is best used as a cold infusion sipped throughout the day. In addition, it is antiseptic and antihemmorhagic, helping to stop bleeding.

Chervil   *Anthriscus cerefolium*

The anise-like aroma and taste of chervil makes it a classic culinary herb. It is usually one of the ingredients of Béarnaise sauce. Native to the Middle East, southern Russia, and the Caucasus, it now grows almost everywhere. Although it is a "spring plant," which goes to seed quickly, it self-seeds well and normally produces a second crop later in the season.

The leaves of this herb lose their flavor quickly, so it is best to use chervil fresh as garnishes or in salads or by adding it just before serving to cooked dishes. Its flavor enhances chicken, fish, vegetable, and egg dishes, as well as salads. It is also good in almost any cream soup.

Like many culinary herbs, chervil assists digestion, but it is not particularly known for its medicinal qualities.

Chives   *Allium schooenoprasum*

With its mild onion-like flavor, chives is used in soups and stews, roasts, meat loafs, and in many salads. It is especially good with potato and egg dishes such as potato salads and omelets. It makes a great garnish for many salads and chicken dishes.

Use the leaves fresh in cooking, generally by simply rinsing and then snipping into short sections, or dry or freeze the snipped leaves for later use. The flowers are showy and they, too, can be eaten, making an attractive addition to salads.

Chives is rarely thought of for its therapeutic value, although the leaves are high in vitamin C, folic acid, and potassium as well as calcium and iron. Due to its sulphur compounds, the plant has medicinal qualities similar to garlic and onion, although to a lesser degree. It also stimulates the appetite and promotes good digestion, contributing to its culinary value.

Chives is a clump forming perennial with slender bulbs, which spread over time. The leaves re-grow after being cut.

Cilantro/Coriander   *Coriandrum sativum*

This is two herbs in one. Cilantro is the herb in its young leafy form before it bolts and flowers. It is one of the oldest known herbs, having been found in ancient Egyptian tombs.

Often an ingredient of salsa, cilantro blends well with other spicy ingredients. Both roots and leaves may be used. Cilantro is popular in Indian and other SE Asian cooking as well as being a staple of Mexican and South American cuisine. Its piquant flavor makes it a great garnish to many foods.

Coriander is the plant in its seed form. It, too, is used in the cuisines of Mexico and South American, as well as Asia. In contrast to cilantro, coriander has a sweet spicy taste. It is used in curries, is a main ingredient of Garam Masala, a favorite Indian spice blend, and is also used in cakes and breads and as a flavoring for liqueurs such as gin and vermouth. It goes well with apples; apple ginger-coriander pie is a special treat.

Cilantro is not particularly noted for its healing value, but aromatherapists use it as an anti-rheumatic. Coriander seeds freshen the breath after eating garlic. Tea made from the seeds helps relieve indigestion.

Cinnamon   *Cinnamomum zeylanicum*

Cinnamon is a favorite for many dishes, especially desserts, breads, and salads. It has a wonderful sweet spiciness and cinnamons from different locations vary from mildly sweet to the supreme sweetness of the Vietnamese variety.

This spice is the ground inner bark of the cinnamon tree native to Sri Lanka and South India, which now proliferates in many areas of SE Asia.

The health value of cinnamon has been known for ages and recently the scientific community has discovered that it lowers LDL cholesterol, helps regulate blood sugar, helps treat and prevent yeast infections, and diminishes arthritic pain. A cup of tea with honey and cinnamon is a morning constitution for many older people, and might well be used by the young, as well. Cinnamon is a great source of manganese, iron, and calcium.

Cumin   *Cuminum cyminum*

Warm, earthy, and pungent, cumin is the dried fruit, although called a seed, of the annual plant, *Cuminum cyminum,* native to the Mediterranean. It now grows in much of the Middle East, southern Russia, China, India, and Turkey. Cumin is well known in the cuisines of these areas. It is also frequently used in Mexican cooking.

Cumin goes well with carrots, chicken, chickpeas, corn, and lamb. It is often found in curry and chili powder as well as in barbecue sauce. It is a common ingredient in soups, stews, curries, casseroles, salsas, and chutneys. It is best to buy cumin as whole dried fruits. Toasting seeds before grinding brings out their flavor. Grind seeds as you use them because, once ground, they lose flavor.

Although not particularly known for medicinal value, cumin allegedly helps cure the common cold, assists digestion, enhances insulin uptake, is anti-inflammatory, and may help prevent cancer. It is rich in calcium, magnesium, iron, zinc, and B vitamins.

Dill   *Anethum graveolens*

Both leaves and seeds of this self-seeding annual plant are used in cooking. Native to Southern Russia, West Africa, and the Mediterranean region, dill is often thought of for its use in pickling.

The tangy leaves, which are harvested in the spring and early summer, are best used fresh, primarily for flavoring soups, sauces and dips, as well as to season fish. Cutting the leaves to use fresh delays dill in going to seed. The seeds, which are more potent, are used in stews and for pickling. Some cultivars produce abundant leaves while others produce fewer leaves and are best used primarily for seed.

Dill is antioxidant and antibacterial. It is a good source of calcium and helps prevent bone loss. Dill leaf is also used to help settle upset stomach and for colicky babies.

Epazote   *Chenopodium ambrosioides*

The pungent leaves of this annual plant native to Mexico and Guatemala add flavor to dried bean dishes, corn, quesadillas, soups, and fish. Epazote is sometimes used in chili and cocktail sauces.

This strong scented herb is best when used fresh, but if dried should be cooked for a period of time to disperse its flavor and soften the dried leaves. Because epazote assists in the digestion of beans, it is not only tasty, but also useful in such dishes.

Fennel seed   *Foeniculum vulgare*

As an herb, the leaves, roots and stems of fennel are used, but some of the recipes in this book call for the warm, sweet anise-like seed that is described here. The English make heavy use of fennel seed in flavoring fish and sausage. Fennell seed is also used in curries and in many curry powders.

Fennel seed aids digestion and helps prevent colic. It dispels flatulence, freshens the breath, and has some anti-microbial action.

Because fennel can pollinate with dill, the two plants should be separated in the garden.

Garlic   *Allium sativum*

Garlic is a staple of cooking in many cuisines from French and

Italian to Asian and South American. It has also become common in much of American cooking. A basic in any pasta, soup, or stew, garlic is also used with beef, chicken, pork, and potato dishes. Garlic toast and bread are common fare.

Garlic has antifungal and antiviral properties. It is expectorant, so is an excellent remedy for colds, flu, and coughs. It promotes sweating, reduces blood pressure, is mildly anticoagulant, and reduces cholesterol and blood sugar. It is a cornucopia of vitamins, minerals, amino acids, and sulphur compounds.

Much of the benefit from garlic comes from a property of its pungent taste. If you remove that flavor, you lose much of the value. To benefit your health, you need to taste the garlic and your friends and family members must tolerate your garlic breath or body odor. Using just some of the herb's extracted constituents limits or eradicates the medicinal effect, which is often the case when using pharmaceutical company herbal preparations.

Garlic cloves should be planted in the fall—October in Minnesota. If you save bulbs for planting, save the largest ones because they produce the biggest bulbs the following year. Mulch heavily with 4-6 inches of straw. Leave the straw on in the spring. The garlic stalks will grow right through it. Harvest garlic when the bottom three leaves turn brown and the soil is reasonably dry.

There are two main varieties of garlic—the soft-neck *(sativum)* often called Italian garlic, and the hard-neck or stiff-neck *(ophioscorodon)*. Soft-neck garlic generally has relatively small cloves with a warm and pungent taste and stiff-necked usually has larger, more full flavored cloves, sometimes with a deep heat. The Italian, which is the most common type, stores better than hard-necked and its soft stems can be braided. Ophio garlic sends up a beautiful globe of tiny lavender flowers. However, the plant generally produces larger bulbs if the stalk is cut back before flowering just after the loop in the stem has appeared.

When cooking with garlic, it is best to add some near the beginning of cooking to infuse its flavor and some at the end of cooking to preserve more of its medicinal value.

Harvest the bulb in mid-late summer. If allowed to dry with good air circulation, many bulbs will last nine months or more.

${\mathcal{G}}$inger   *Zingibar officinale*

Ginger is integral to Chinese, Indian, and other Asian cuisines, where it is native. It is used in curries and chutneys and is almost always an ingredient in curry powders. The fresh ginger rhizome, which is the ideal way to use this herb, is sweet, warm, and pungent. As a powder, ginger is often an ingredient of breads, desserts, and cookies.

Fresh ginger is always peeled before use in cooking. It is fibrous, so for most dishes it's best to mince finely or grate, although small slivers can add a wonderful chewy zest. For broths, soups, and stews, fresh ginger slices are often used, but should be removed before serving. If powdered ginger is substituted for fresh, use only about ⅛ the amount.

Ginger stores well in the refrigerator, wrapped in a paper towel and then put into a plastic bag. It may also be frozen by peeling, slicing, and placing it in a plastic bag. Prepared the same way, it may also be preserved by putting it in rice wine or sherry.

The use of this herb spread to many ancient cultures and it was one of the herbs used to fight the Bubonic Plague in Europe. It was also used as an aphrodisiac. Ginger ale developed as a result of barkeepers putting out powdered ginger to use in beer.

Ginger increases the flow of saliva and digestive juices, so is a good digestive aid. It diminishes motion sickness, helps expel phlegm and to remove toxins through the liver, and is anti-inflammatory. It is full of essential and medicinal nutrients.

${\mathcal{L}}$avender   *Lavendula angustifolia*

Lavender is making a comeback in the culinary arts. The aromatic flowers add a slightly sweet and citrus-like flavor to sauces for meat and fish dishes, an attractive addition to salads, and can be substituted for rosemary in most recipes. Lavender is also used in decorating desserts and makes a striking and delicious jelly. English lavender is sweeter than French and is best for cooking . However, it should be used sparingly or its perfume-like taste will be unpleasant.

Lavender, native to the Middle East, is an ancient herb that was used for mummification and perfumery. It quickly spread throughout Europe as civilizations moved westward. Sunny conditions are necessary for it to flower well. Harvest the flowers near the end of flowering during the heat of the noonday sun.

Lavender is a relaxing, uplifting herb that is said to bring a peaceful state of mind and to relieve headaches and hoarseness as well as soothe sore joints.

Lemon verbena   *Aloysia triplylla*

Native to Chile, lemon verbena has a wonderful lemon scent and taste. When walking through the garden, there is almost nothing better than picking a lemon verbena leaf, rubbing it, and inhaling the aroma. The leaves retain their aroma well even when dried. It is rarely used in cooking, but the fresh leaves, snipped finely, add a fresh zest to salads or, used whole, to teas and alcoholic drinks.

Although seldom used medicinally, lemon verbena helps relieve digestive spasms, reduces fever, and has a mild sedative effect. It is bactericidal so is good for mild illnesses. Whether used medically or not, it makes a wonderfully refreshing tisane and is a nice addition to other herbal teas. The essential oil is used in aromatherapy for stress and to improve liver function.

In colder zones, lemon verbena rarely survives winters, so is best grown as a container plant or as an annual. Harvest leaves throughout the growing season. The leaves dry readily, either in the dehydrator at 105 degrees or hung to dry.

Lovage   *Levisticum officinale*

A hardy spreading perennial, lovage leaves are best used in the springtime before their flavor becomes bitter. Traditionally this herb has been used in the cuisines of southern Europe. Spring leaves have a bright, pungent aroma and taste and are especially appealing in salads and soups.

No extravagant claims have been made for the medicinal quality of lovage, but it is said to stimulate digestion and is antiseptic. It is high in quercetin, which is touted as a cancer preventative.

Mint

Mentha piperita, spicata, etc.

Peppermint, apple mint, spearmint, lavender mint, chocolate mint, English mint, and others assist digestion by helping to relax muscles of the digestive tract and by stimulating bile flow, thus are healthful aids to many dishes and beverages. However, for indigestion caused by a weak sphincter muscle causing acid reflux, the mints are not helpful because of their tendency to relax the diaphragmatic muscle.

The menthol in mints is antiseptic, decongestant, and analgesic and gives them their typical smell and taste. Mints also promote sweating in fevers.

English mint is the best to use in cooking peas, lamb, potatoes, and for mint jelly and mint juleps, while peppermint is the most beneficial for digestion. Mint adds a fresh taste to fruit salads and is a nice addition to salad dressings, especially dressings used for fruit. Indian and SE Asian cooking make heavy use of mint in such dishes as tabbuleh and with lamb.

Most mints spread by their roots and will invade much of the garden space around them, so it is best to plant them in pots or in gardens separate from other plants. All are aromatic and have square stems. They grow wild and have been heavily hybridized, so identification is often difficult. Harvest the leaves before flowering for the best taste and most volatile oil.

Mustard

Brassica alba, nigra & juncea

Warm, pungent mustard seeds, ranging from white to brown, come from the various varieties of the *Brassica* family. Ground mustard seeds are common in many condiments, as well as in baked beans, deviled eggs, potato salads, many meat dishes, and various pickles. In general, the white seeds are relatively mild and the brown ones sharper and stronger.

Ground mustard seed is also mixed with vinegar, wine, other spices, and sometimes sugar or honey to make what is commonly called "mustard."

As a medicine, mustard is high in sulphur and the seeds have been used for venomous insect stings, poultices for inflamed muscles, respiratory ills, and as appetite and circulatory stimulants.

Nasturtium

Tropaeolum majus/minus

Nasturtium flowers are edible and high in vitamin C. They make attractive garnishes for salads, pastas, and other dishes. The leaves have a peppery flavor and can serve as a pepper substitute. Both leaves and flowers add flavor, health benefits, and color to herbal vinegars.

Nasturtium provides energy, conditions the skin and hair, increases resistance to fungal and bacterial infections, and helps clear excess mucus. Both flowers and leaves may be dried for use in cooking or in herbal tisanes or teas.

Nasturtium is a pretty garden flower with a variety of colors. *Tropaeolum majus* is a climber with vines reaching up to six feet, while *Tropaeolum minus* grows about twelve inches high and is ideal in borders, window boxes, and hanging baskets.

This plant grows best in poor to moderate soils because very rich soils make it produce more leaves than flowers. It is beneficial to plant nasturtium near cucumbers because it deters cucumber beetles. Planting near the base of apple trees may deter aphids from attacking the trees.

Onion
Allium cepa

There are about seven hundred species of onions, which are universally used as vegetables, flavorings, and for medicine. They are ingredients in most meat dishes, in salads, soups, stews, and even breads.

From the sweet, mild taste of Vidalia and Candy onions, to the wonderful aroma and pungency of red onions, to the eye-watering sharpness of long-storage varieties such as Copra, onions add both flavor and health to most meals.

Sulphur compounds create the odor of onions as well as much of the medicinal action that helps to protect against infection. Onion tea is a good remedy for symptoms of the common cold. Onions also help reduce blood pressure and slightly diminish clotting time and blood sugar. They are expectorant and diuretic.

This plant is biennial, producing various sized bulbs. Most often, however, onions are planted from small plants and grown as annuals.

Oregano
Origanum vulgare

Origanum vulgare is sometimes called wild marjoram, which is distinct from sweet marjorum, *Origanum majorana.* Commercially dried oregano is usually made from Greek or Turkish oregano, *Origanum vulgare* subspecies *hirtum,* or from Mexican oregano, which is not truly of the *origanum* genus. Oregano grown in southern climates is generally more flavorful than that grown in northern climates.

Oregano is one of the few herbs in which the pungency increases with drying. Used primarily for cooking, it is good with strong flavors such as chili, pizza, and Greek, Italian, and Mexican cooking.

As a medicine, *Origanum vulgare* helps relieve symptoms of coughs, colds, and mild feverish illnesses.

A hardy perennial, *Oreganum vulgare* likes sunny conditions in well drained alkaline soils. Some other varieties are not as hardy. The plant gradually spreads in the garden and generally produces purple or pink flowers in panicles, with some varieties producing white flowers. Because there are so many varieties and hybrids, identification is often difficult.

Paprika   *Capsicum annuum*

There are many varieties of the pepper plant, *Capsicum annuum*, ranging from the hot cayenne to the sweet bells. Paprika is one such cultivar and it too has types that vary from quite mild and sweet to the warm, but slightly sweet, Hungarian variety.

Paprika used in cooking is the dried, ground fruit of the plant. Its bright orange to red color often tints cheese and garnishes deviled eggs and hors d'ouvres. Paprika is also used for fish and chicken dishes and in stews and vegetables.

Rich in beta-carotene and vitamin C, which is preserved if the pepper is dried appropriately at temperatures not higher than 117°, paprika also assists digestion and circulation.

Parsley   *Petroselium crispus*

Parsley originated in the eastern Mediterranean region and has been known as a medicinal herb for more than two thousand years.

Flat-leaved, or Italian, parsley leaves are good flavorings for sauces, butter, dressings, stuffings, salads, meatloaf, and almost any meat-based or vegetable dish. They are a main ingredient of tabbouleh, a Middle Eastern dish. For a tasty appetizer, spread parsley pesto (recipe in miscellaneous/appetizer section) on crackers or baguettes.

Flat-leaved parsley is an excellent potassium sparing diuretic that accelerates the excretion of toxins. It burns excess fat, helps contract the uterus after childbearing, and is antiseptic for the urinary tract, so helps prevent and treat infections. Eaten fresh, parsley freshens the breath.

Flat-leaved parsley tea reputedly helps dissolve kidney stones. In addition, it strengthens the digestive system. It contains vitamins A and C as well as several minerals. The root is more medicinal than the leaves for the above conditions, although the leaves have a higher concentration of the vitamins and minerals. Flat-leaved parsley is more flavorful and medicinal than the curly type, which is better known. The curly type is used primarily as a garnish.

Parsley grows well from seed planted in early spring in a sunny, well drained garden and lasts late into the fall, withstanding early frosts. It is harvested from mid-summer until the frost finally kills it. Germination may be a little spotty, so it is best to over-plant and thin as necessary. It is also helpful to soak the seeds in warm water before sowing.

Rosemary   *Rosemarinus officinalis*

One of the major herbs used in Italian dishes, rosemary makes a great flavoring for poultry and pork as well. It is especially good mixed with olive oil and spread under the skin when roasting a chicken—or put a sprig on a chicken breast when sautéing it.

Rosemary is a favorite for both culinary and medicinal use. It is especially valuable for strengthening the heart, therefore limiting or preventing cardiac hypertrophy and eventual heart failure. In addition, rosemary, like most culinary herbs, is antimicrobial—especially antifungal and antibacterial. It helps eliminate the bacteria that cause tooth decay. It also helps digest fats and oils, so is useful in pasta dishes that may include cream, cheese, or oils. In history, rosemary is associated with memory and fidelity. It is a mild pain killer and sedative, so helps relieve headaches and anxiety induced indigestion.

Rosemary is an aromatic perennial shrub in southern areas, but grows only as an annual in northern zones. It will not grow from seed, at least not during a season, so small plants should be put out in spring. It needs full sun and likes dry conditions. Mulch to prevent dirt splashing on the plant because it is difficult to clean it off. .Harvest rosemary's leaves throughout the growing season. They dry easily either by hanging with good air circulation or in a dehydrator at 105 degrees.

Sage   *Salvia officinalis*

Sage and onion, traditionally used in poultry stuffing, aid the digestion of fats and oils, so are especially useful in sausage and in pork, geese, and duck dishes, but of course are great with turkey, chicken, and lamb, as well. Many soups benefit from sage and it is even good, chopped finely, in grilled cheese sandwiches.

Garden sage is even more important as a medicinal herb than for its culinary value. Since antiquity, it has been believed to produce a long life. A thirteenth century verse says, "Why should a man die, whilst Sage grows in his garden?"

Traditional use of sage for medicine in this country was for sores in the mouth and sore throats. Sage tea was also used for fevers and nervous or brain diseases. It was used then and is used now for menopausal hot flashes, painful joints, tension headaches, and palsy or Parkinson's disease. The volatile oils of this herb are strongly antiseptic, anti-inflammatory, and anti-microbial. Some evidence suggests that an enzyme in sage may protect against Alzheimer's and other dementias.

There are many varieties of garden sage, some with white flowers, others with purple or pink ones. Seeds may be sown in the spring, but it is advantageous to buy small plants or use cuttings or divisions. This herb is perennial, but usually dies out after a few years. Mulch it for winter and prune back heavily in spring.

Snip fresh leaves as desired throughout the season. Gather in full sun to best preserve the volatile oils. Usually you'll still be able to take some fresh leaves at Thanksgiving in Minnesota. They'll taste good, but will not look as appealing as earlier in the season. Sage dries well when hung to dry, but using a dehydrator at about 100 degrees better preserves the oil and color.

Savory

Satureja hortensis (summer savory)
Satureja Montana (winter savory)

Synonymous with "tasty," savory leaves are a common flavoring for green vegetables, especially beans. Summer savory, an annual, is more delicate in flavor and is often used in cooking fresh green beans, whereas winter savory, a perennial, adds a peppery spiciness to longer cooking dishes such as dried beans, stews and soups.

Savory aids the digestion of legumes, which is why it is often found in bean dishes, and assists digestion in general. It is also antiseptic and is sometimes found in homemade soap recipes and commercial soaps.

Star anise

Illicium verum

Distinct from anise (*Pimpinella anisus*), star anise is the star-shaped fruit/seed pod of *Illicium*. More pungent than anise seed. It is native to southwest China and common to recipes from China and India for flavoring meats, stocks, and soups . It is also used to flavor the liquor Galliano.

Similar to anise seed, it has digestive and expectorant qualities and help freshen breath. An ingredient in this spice was used in developing the antiviral medication, Tamiflu.

Stinging nettles

Urtica dioeca/urens

Stinging nettle is not considered a culinary herb. However, this plant is full of nutrients, including vitamins and minerals, especially Vitamin C and iron, and is high in protein. The Europeans brought stinging nettles with them to America to protect them from scurvy.

Nettles is used primarily in soups and casseroles and as a spinach substitute. It is one of the first plants to emerge in spring and should be harvested when it is just 4-8 inches high. Using it fresh is best, but nettles retains its nutrient qualities frozen as well. When dried, it loses some of its value.

The tiny hairs along the stems of stinging nettles produce formic acid and give a "sting" to the skin if you touch the growing plant or within an hour or so after harvesting. Therefore, use care and gloves when harvesting. Cooking destroys the stinging quality.

Tarragon   *Artemisia dracunculus sativa*

Tarragon is excellent with chicken dishes as well as with salmon and other fish. It has an anise or licorice-like flavor. Famous sauces such as Béarnaise and hollandaise contain this herb. While tarragon is wonderful to use fresh, it is almost as flavorful when preserved in vinegar.

Tarragon was called a "dragon herb" because of its use for venomous stings and snake bites, but it is generally not used medicinally today; however, it does stimulate digestion and, as with all artemisias, helps expel intestinal worms.

Dark green shiny leaves grow on this shrubby plant, which reaches about three feet high. It is best harvested in the spring and very early summer. The taste diminishes and the size of leaves becomes smaller as the season progresses. Tarragon requires light, well drained soil in a sunny location, and is very hardy.

Harvest the leaves for cooking. To dry them, use early spring tarragon, the oils of which are more intense than those from tarragon harvested later. To dry, remove the leaves from the stem, place on dehydrator trays, and dry at 100 degrees. However, drying is not as effective at retaining flavor as freezing or preserving in vinegar. The leaves should remain on the stem for freezing or making vinegars.

Thyme   *Thymus vulgaris*

Generally considered a culinary herb, thyme is also one of the most medicinal herbs. In cooking, it adds a robust savory flavor to fowl, soups, and stews. It is a traditional seasoning, along with sage, for turkey dressing. Thyme, especially lemon thyme, seasons fish well.

It strengthens the lungs and helps open the air pathways,

mostly by reducing phlegm, and is reputed to retard the aging process. It is antiviral, antifungal, and expectorant and has been used in the treatment of bronchitis, whooping cough, and other chest infections. Thymol, the essential oil in thyme, is strongly antiseptic and is used as a mouthwash and in toothpaste as well as to control varroa mites in honey bees. Thyme tea is excellent for use during colds and influenza.

The Abbess Hildegard von Bingen, who lived during the 12th century said, "He who drinks a cup of thyme tea instead of coffee in the morning will soon feel the beneficial effect: enlivened spirits, great comfort in the stomach, no coughing in the morning and an overall well-being."

There are many varieties of thyme, including French and English as well as the hybrid flavor types such as lemon thyme. It is a slow growing short plant with tiny leaves and even tinier flowers, ideal for containers. The leaves are best harvested before flowering and picked in the noonday sun.

For harvest the same season, begin with small plants rather than seeds. Thyme needs full sun and good drainage. Winter wet can cause rot, which causes it to die. To prevent this, put gravel right under the plant and do not mulch, in spite of the fact that severe winters can take their toll. In their native warmer climates in Europe and Asia, thymes grow as perennial shrubs or evergreens.

Turmeric   *Curcuma domestica*

Another ancient spice, turmeric originated in SE Asia. Due to its deep yellow coloring, it was often used as a dye.

Turmeric is usually available ground and is a common ingredient in the cuisines of the Far and Middle East. In India, it is often used to tint cakes and other sweet dishes. It is also used to spice meat, especially lamb, as well as for vegetables. Like ginger, it is usually found in curry powders and in most curry recipes.

This spice is well known as an anti-inflammatory, but is also anti-bacterial and assists digestion.

~~~~~

$\mathcal{S}$uggestions regarding recipe ingredients

$\mathcal{I}$n almost all recipes, **use fresh or frozen herbs whenever possible. Substitute with dried herbs, using one-fourth to one-third as much, when fresh are not available**. An exception is ginger. Except for breads and pastries, it is best to use fresh ginger, usually peeled and grated; however, if you substitute with powdered ginger, use about ⅛ as much ground as you would fresh.

When herbs such as thyme, rosemary, and tarragon are called for in recipes, it is the stripped leaves that are used, unless the recipe calls for "sprigs." With herbs such as cilantro that have soft stems, some of the stem material may be used as well.

When a recipe calls for olive oil, use extra virgin oil, especially for salads and dressings when it will not by heated. Keep it fresh in the refrigerator after opening. When vegetable, beef, or chicken stock is an ingredient, use homemade stock when possible, made when you have a chicken or turkey carcass, beef bones with a little meat remaining, or extra vegetables. When using store-bought canned broth, use lower-sodium varieties.

For both best taste and health purposes, butter is preferable to margarine or other spreads. Although these spreads have been promoted as healthier, the artificial hydrogenation of the fats creates an unnatural product that our bodies have difficulty metabolizing. Butter, used in moderation, is healthier since it has nutritional benefits such as enhancing the absorption of hormones and other nutrients. Over the millennia, our bodies evolved with its use, and developed physiology to manage its cholesterol content. Nonetheless, butter should be used in limited quantities. Olive oil is preferable for sautéing most items.

Using butter from grass-fed cows not only provides better

taste than from most commercial butters, but is a healthier choice and supports a rural industry that raises animals in a humane manner. Similarly, eggs from free-range chickens, beef from grass-fed cattle, and pork from pasture-fed pigs are good choices. The eggs from free-range chickens have more of the healthy omega 3 fat. You can see that the yolks are a much deeper yellow than those from cage-raised hens. Grass-fed, pastured animals live happy, natural lives and eat the food their physiology demands for passing on healthy attributes to you.

Be careful not to overcook pasture-fed meat and poultry. Heat for slightly less time than for other meats and at somewhat reduced temperatures. **The internal temperature recommendations for beef, pork, and poultry in this publication assume grass-fed or pasture-raised animals.** Remember that while your meat is resting after removing from cooking, the internal temperature will increase five degrees or so. **For non-grass-fed meat, use slightly higher oven temperatures, longer cooking times, and slightly higher internal temperatures than those recommended in this book.**

In the current culture, you receive sufficient iodine from salt added to most prepared and restaurant-served foods, so use sea salt at home when you can. Our bodies have adapted to sea salt over millennia. It contains essential minerals that sodium chloride does not. Remember, too, when cooking with herbs that add so much flavor, minimal salt is needed. In the recipes that follow, the use of the word "salt" means finely ground sea salt unless specified otherwise, for which you may substitute table salt 1:1.

Because there are many so-called Parmesan cheeses that are imitations, I have used the designation, Parmigiano, to describe *Parmigiano-Reggiano* cheese, which is the Italian word for the French *Parmesan* .

Finally, remember that you need not follow most recipes exactly. Substitute liberally with ingredients that you have available and that may enhance the flavor or contribute to the dish just as well as those listed, or perhaps better.

Enjoy and stay healthy!

BREADS

CHEESE & HERB BISCUITS

Ingredients:
- 3 cups all-purpose flour
- 3 teaspoons baking powder
- ¾ teaspoon baking soda
- ¾ teaspoon salt
- ¾ cup cold butter, cut up
- ⅓ cup fresh or frozen chives, snipped
- 1 teaspoon fresh oregano, chopped (or substitute your favorite herb)
- ¾ cup cheddar, Swiss, Asiago or your favorite cheese, grated
- 1 cup buttermilk

Preheat oven to 375°.

Mix dry ingredients. Blend in butter until texture is fine. Stir in cheese and herbs.

Add buttermilk and mix until dry ingredients are moistened.

Knead dough 1-2 minutes.

Pat dough into 1inch thick square.

Cut dough into 12 square pieces and place on parchment lined or lightly greased baking sheet; alternatively, fit into muffin pan or biscuit pan.

Bake about 20 minutes until golden brown.

CASSEROLE POTATO BREAD WITH HERBS

Ingredients:
- 1 large red potato, boiled and mashed
- Water from boiled potatoes, cooled to lukewarm, with additional water added as needed to make 1 cup
- 3½ cups all-purpose flour
- 1½ teaspoons salt
- 1 teaspoon sugar
- 1 tablespoon yeast
- 3 tablespoons olive oil, divided
- 1 egg, slightly beaten
- 1 teaspoon fresh basil, finely chopped
- 1 teaspoon fresh oregano, finely chopped
- 1 teaspoon fresh rosemary, finely chopped
- 1 teaspoon garlic powder (optional)

¾ cup combination of mozzarella, Asiago, and Parmigiano cheeses, or your favorite cheese, divided
Corn meal or flour to dust pan
1 teaspoon medium grind sea salt

Mix 2 cups flour and salt in large bowl. Create a crater in the center. Put yeast and sugar into center of bowl; add warm potato water. Allow yeast to begin bubbling, about 5-8 minutes.
Mix flour into liquid.
Add 2 tablespoons oil, herbs, mashed potato, egg, and ⅔ cup cheese. Mix well.
Add remaining 1½ cups flour, ½ cup at a time.
Knead until smooth and elastic, adding up to ¼ cup more flour if necessary to make an elastic, but slightly sticky dough.
Place in oiled bowl and cover. Let rise until double, usually ½-1 hour.
Punch dough down and shape into round loaf.
Place in greased baking pan, with corn meal or flour sprinkled in the bottom. (An 8-inch square or round pan works well.)
Let rise until double.
Preheat oven to 350°.
Spread remaining tablespoon olive oil over dough. Sprinkle with sea salt and remaining cheese.
Bake 35 minutes or until nicely browned.
Serve warm, ideally with a mixture of olive oil, herbs, and balsamic vinegar.

This recipe can also be used for pizza crust, but potato and egg should be left out and warm water substituted for potato water.
For the final rising, it should be spread on pizza pan about ¼ inch thick and let to rise just 15 minutes.

HERB DINNER ROLLS

Ingredients:
- 1 cup warm milk
- 1 tablespoon yeast
- 1 tablespoon honey
- 1 tablespoon olive oil
- 1¾ cup all-purpose flour
- ½ cup whole wheat flour
- 1 teaspoon fresh rosemary, finely chopped
- 1 teaspoon fresh thyme
- 1 teaspoon fresh oregano, finely chopped
- ½ teaspoon salt
- ¼ teaspoon black pepper, or to taste
- Small amount milk

Heat milk to lukewarm. Mix in yeast, honey, and oil. Let stand 4-5 minutes.

In large bowl, add 1 cup all-purpose flour and wheat flour, herbs, salt, and pepper. Mix well.

Knead in final ¾ cup all-purpose flour and continue kneading until mixture sticks together well.

Place dough in oiled bowl. Cover with light cloth and let rise in warm place until double.

Punch down and turn out onto floured surface.

Roll to 16-18 inches long. Cut into 12 pieces and roll each into a ball.

Preheat oven to 400°.

Place each ball of dough on greased or lined baking sheet, leaving about 2 inches between pieces.

Cover with towel and let rise 15 minutes or until nearly double.

Lightly brush the balls with milk.

Bake for 15-20 minutes or until lightly browned.

HERBED GARLIC BREAD

Ingredients:
- 2 large cloves garlic, minced
- 3 tablespoons olive oil
- 2 tablespoons fresh parsley, chopped

1 tablespoon fresh thyme
2 teaspoons fresh oregano, finely chopped
½ teaspoon paprika
2 tablespoons Parmigiano or Romano cheese, grated
Baked large loaf of French or Italian bread or two small loaves

Preheat oven to 350°.
Pound garlic in mortar with pestle. Add olive oil and mix well, or mix in
    small blender.
In small bowl combine herbs. Add cheese and mix well.
Cut bread crosswise into diagonal slices without cutting all the way
    through. Brush bread with garlic oil. Sprinkle herb/cheese mixture
    between slices.
Wrap bread in foil.
Place on baking sheet. Bake 10-15 minutes.
Serve immediately.

LIGHT HERB BREAD

Ingredients:
    Dough from your favorite recipe for 2 loaves white or light wheat bread
    ⅓ cup butter
    1 teaspoon fresh basil, chopped
    1 teaspoon fresh rosemary, chopped
    2 tablespoons fresh flat-leaved parsley, chopped
    3 medium cloves garlic, finely minced
    1 teaspoon olive oil

Prepare your favorite bread recipe.
Grease 2 loaf pans
After bread has been through first rise, snip into walnut size pieces and
    arrange in loaf pans.
Combine remaining ingredients and sprinkle over dough.
Cover and let rise until double, about 1½ hours
In the meantime, preheat oven to 375°.
Bake until slightly browned, about 30-35 minutes.
Let cool in pans for 10 minutes before removing.

SLOW-RISE LEMON HERB BREAD

An artisan bread, great with soups and salads, that
requires 16 or more hours to finish

Ingredients:
  3 cups all-purpose flour
  1 scant teaspoon active dry yeast
  1½ teaspoons salt
  2 teaspoons fresh rosemary, finely
      chopped
  1 teaspoon lemon thyme or dill
      weed
  2 teaspoons lemon zest
  1½ cups water
  1 tablespoon freshly squeezed
      lemon juice

Combine flour, yeast, salt, herbs, and zest in large bowl.

Add lemon juice to water, then add slowly to flour mixture, mixing until all
    the dough is sticky.

Cover with plastic wrap and let rise 12-18 hours until bubbly on top.

Place dough on floured surface and work just slightly. Shape into a ball.

Coat a "flour sack" towel with cornmeal. Place dough in center of towel
    and cover with rest of towel.

Let rise 2-3 hours until about double.

Preheat oven to 450° toward end of time while bread is rising.

Place cast iron or other ovenproof pot in oven for 20-30 minutes before
    bread is ready to bake.

Using pot holders, remove pot and turn bread into ungreased hot pot.

Cover pot and return to oven and bake 30 minutes.

Remove cover and bake another 20 minutes or so until bread is browned,
    then remove from oven.

Let bread cool in pot for 10 minutes, then turn bread out. (It will come out
    easily.)

WHEAT ZUCCHINI HERB BREAD

Ingredients:
- 2½ cups bread flour
- 1 teaspoon salt
- 1 cup whole wheat flour
- 1 tablespoon yeast
- 2 teaspoons olive oil
- ¾ cup warm water
- 1 tablespoon honey
- 1 cup zucchini, peeled and sliced
- 1 teaspoon fresh rosemary, finely chopped
- 1 teaspoon fresh basil, finely chopped
- 1 tablespoon sesame seeds

Mix 1 cup bread flour, salt, wheat flour, and yeast. Add honey, water, and oil. Mix lightly.

Add zucchini and herbs. Mix well.

Add remaining bread flour, ½ cup at a time, and knead until dough sticks together well.

Let rise ½ hour or until double.

Punch down. Shape into loaf and place in greased loaf pan.

Let rise until double.

When bread is almost risen, preheat oven to 350°.

Bake for 35-40 minutes or until bread sounds hollow when hit with fingers.

Remove from pan immediately after baking. Cool.

*MOM'S CARDAMOM CHRISTMAS BREAD

Ingredients:
    1½ tablespoons dry yeast
    ⅓ cup lukewarm water
    1 teaspoon sugar
    1¼ cups milk, scalded
    ¼ cup honey
    ¼ cup sugar
    1 teaspoon salt
    1 cup butter, softened
    5½-6 cups white flour (I use bread flour, but Mom used all-purpose.)
    2 eggs, lightly beaten
    2 teaspoons cardamom seed, ground
    1 egg white, beaten with 1 teaspoon water

Dissolve yeast in water with sugar. Let stand until foamy.

Mix scalded milk with honey, sugar, salt, and butter. Cool to lukewarm, then add to yeast alternately with 2 cups flour. Beat.

Add eggs and cardamom and mix well.

Stir in remaining flour to make a soft dough. Knead until smooth and elastic.

Place in greased bowl and turn over once. Let rise until double.

Punch dough down and knead lightly.

Divide dough into 6 sections. Roll each section to a rope about 1 foot long.

Using 3 ropes, pinch ends together, then braid and pinch far ends together. Tuck ends under. Repeat for second braid. Place on greased baking sheet.

Let rise until double.

Preheat oven to 350° while dough is rising.

Brush top of loaves with egg white mixture.

Bake about 30 minutes until golden brown.

Excellent served warm with butter and jam

*   *I had three recipes for cardamom bread and I think this is my mom's, but am not certain.*

MEAT & FISH

BEEF

BEEF STEAK WITH CHERRIES & ROSEMARY

Ingredients:
>   2-pound top beef round steak or sirloin steak (or cube steaks)
>   Port—enough to marinade beef and to have 1½ cups after marinating
>   1 sprig rosemary, leaves removed and
>   chopped
>   1 cup dried cherries
>   1½ cups beef broth
>   3 tablespoons cornstarch
>   Salt and pepper to taste
>   ½ cup all-purpose flour
>   3 tablespoons olive oil
>   1 tablespoon butter
>   ¾ cup chopped red onion
>   3 tablespoons fresh rosemary, chopped
>   ⅓ cup balsamic vinegar
>   Parsley or rosemary sprigs for garnish

Prepare beef by removing from bone, if necessary, cutting into serving size pieces, and pounding to about ¼ inch thick.

Sprinkle a little chopped rosemary on each piece of beef and place beef in a bowl.

Just barely cover beef with port and marinade a few hours.

After beef is marinated, drain port into measuring cup and add enough port to make 1½ cups.

Combine port and cherries in saucepan.

Bring to boil and simmer 5 minutes. Remove from heat.

Whisk broth and cornstarch until smooth.

Season beef with salt and pepper. Dredge in flour.

Heat oil in large skillet. Add half the beef cutlets, brown, and just cook through, about 4 minutes per side.

Transfer to platter and keep warm while browning and cooking the rest.

Transfer remaining cutlets to plate.

Put butter in pan. Add onion and rosemary and cook a few minutes until onion is tender and golden.

Whisk cornstarch mixture into pan. Add cherry mixture and vinegar. Heat until bubbly.

Add beef to sauce and cook until heated through, about 2-3 minutes.

Garnish with fresh parsley or a sprig or 2 of rosemary.

BEEF TENDERLOIN WITH THYME & WINE SAUCE

For a family gathering or a group

Ingredients for roasting beef:
    1 beef tenderloin, about 5 pounds
    Coarse ground sea salt and pepper
    15-20 sprigs fresh thyme

Ingredients for wine sauce:
    5 tablespoons butter
    2 large leeks
    2 cups dry red wine
    2 tablespoons red wine vinegar
    3 cans consommé soup (or homemade beef broth, boiled down to half)
    1 teaspoon fresh thyme
    1 tablespoon butter for whisking into completed sauce

Heat oven to 250°.

Season tenderloin with salt and pepper.

Using twine, tie up tenderloin, making a roast of fairly even thickness.

Put thyme sprigs over tenderloin, tucking some of the sprigs beneath twine.

Place tenderloin in roasting pan and roast until beef is 130-135°, 2-2½ hours.

Meanwhile, about one hour after putting meat in oven, melt butter in pan. Add leeks and cook about 10 minutes on medium heat until golden, but not deeply browned.

Add wine and vinegar, turning heat to high, and reduce by half.

Add consommé or broth and fresh thyme leaves and cook 3-4 minutes. Let sit until roast is done.

Remove roast from pan when temperature in correct. Keep warm for 10 minutes, then remove thyme sprigs before carving.

Re-heat sauce, adding 1 tablespoon butter.

Serve roast covered with sauce, with additional sauce available to ladle.

HERB RUBBED BEEF ROAST WITH ROASTED POTATOES

Ingredients:
    1 pound potatoes (your favorite), cut into large chunks
    ¼ cup flat-leaved parsley, coarsely chopped
    1 teaspoon each: fresh rosemary, oregano, and thyme, chopped
    2 large cloves garlic, coarsely chopped
    2 teaspoons coarse sea salt
    2 tablespoons olive oil
    3-pound eye of the round or sirloin tip beef roast, seasoned with
        salt and pepper
    Zest of ½ lemon

Preheat oven to 325°.
Parboil potatoes for 15 minutes. Drain, reserving water for gravy.
Combine all herbs, garlic and sea salt in mortar. Crush and mix with pestle
    (or use small blender).
Heat olive oil in large skillet. Sear roast on all sides until brown.
Remove roast to roasting pan. Surround with par-boiled potatoes.
Rub herb mixture into top of beef.
Sprinkle roast and potatoes with lemon zest.
Roast in oven until beef is about 135° (about 2 hours).
Let rest 10-15 minutes before carving.

SHORT RIBS IN TOMATO HERB SAUCE

Ingredients:
    5-6 pounds beef short ribs
    Salt and pepper to taste, using plenty of salt
    2-3 tablespoons olive oil
    Carrots (however many you like), chopped
    2 onions, chopped
    1 rib celery, chopped
    1 bulb garlic, separated into cloves, with cloves left whole
    1 tablespoon fresh basil, coarsely chopped
    1 tablespoon fresh thyme
    1 tablespoon fresh summer savory

1 tablespoon fresh oregano
Any other herbs you like and have on hand
¼ cup all-purpose flour
2 cups red wine
1 10½-ounce can consommé soup (or beef broth reduced by one-half)
1 quart canned tomatoes or 3-4 fresh tomatoes, coarsely chopped

Preheat oven to 300°.
Season ribs with salt and pepper and set aside.
Heat oil in ovenproof pot. Brown ribs. Set aside on plate.
Add carrots, onions, and celery to pan drippings, cooking until tender.
Add garlic, herbs, and flour. Stir well.
Gradually add wine, stirring constantly, then add consommé or broth.
Boil briefly. Add tomatoes and boil 1-2 minutes.
Add ribs, cover and bake in oven for about four hours or put in slow cooker
    on low for 8-10 hours until ribs are very tender.

SLOW COOKED BEEF ROAST WITH HERBS & VEGETABLES

A tasty, nutritious family dinner that cooks itself
while you enjoy activities with your family

Ingredients:

Chuck, rump, or round roast, 4-5 pounds
Salt and pepper to taste
2 tablespoons olive oil
1½ pounds carrots, thickly sliced
2-3 onions, thinly sliced
2 ribs celery, chopped
1 green pepper, chopped
1 pint canned tomatoes or 2-3 tomatoes, cut up
4 medium cloves garlic, each chopped into several pieces or slices
4 sprigs thyme
6 sprigs flat-leaved parsley
2 bay leaves
½ cup beef broth or water
½ cup dry red wine or red wine vinegar
6-8 medium potatoes, scrubbed but not peeled, and cut in half
Fresh or frozen vegetables of your choice, such as green beans or corn
(optional)

Heat olive oil in large skillet.
Season roast with salt and pepper, then brown meat on all sides.
Put roast in large slow cooker.
Cover with chopped vegetables and garlic.
Tie herbs in cheesecloth and add to pot to remove later (or strip leaves
from stems before adding directly).
Pour water or broth and vinegar or wine over vegetables.
Cook on low heat 5-6 hours or until meat is tender.
Remove herbs in cheesecloth bag.
Add potatoes as well as more water or broth if needed.
Cook another 1-1½ hours until potatoes are cooked through and meat is
fork tender, adding vegetables, if using, about 20 minutes before
cooking time is done.

CHICKEN

BAKED CHICKEN WITH HERBS & LEMON

Ingredients:
- 2 large cloves garlic
- 1 teaspoon coarse sea salt
- 3 tablespoons olive oil
- Black pepper to taste
- 1 teaspoon fresh rosemary
- ½ teaspoon fresh thyme or sage, finely minced
- 1 large chicken, cut into pieces
- 1 lemon, cut into several wedges
- A few sprigs of fresh rosemary, thyme, or sage or all three
- Parsley to garnish, if desired

Pound garlic with salt, using a mortar and pestle if available.

Add oil slowly and mix until well blended. Add herbs and blend to form a paste.

Rub paste all over chicken pieces, including under skin where possible.

Refrigerate chicken for several hours or overnight.

Preheat oven to 375°.

Arrange chicken pieces in shallow baking dish.

Squeeze lemon pieces slightly, dripping lemon on chicken; then place lemon pieces on top of chicken.

Place fresh herb sprigs on chicken.

Bake about 1 hour until chicken juices run clear.

Remove lemon pieces and herb sprigs.

Place chicken on serving platter. Drizzle pan drippings over chicken.

Add a few herb sprigs or some fresh parsley to garnish.

CHICKEN BREAST CUTLETS IN TOMATO SAUCE

Ingredients for preparing chicken:
- 4 boneless chicken breasts
- ¼ cup all-purpose flour
- Salt and pepper to taste
- 2 tablespoons olive oil

Ingredients for sauce:
- 1 leek, thinly sliced
- 1 medium clove garlic, minced
- ½ cup dry white wine
- 3 fresh tomatoes, diced
- 2 tablespoons fresh basil, chopped
- 1 teaspoon fresh rosemary, cut up
- 1 teaspoon fresh oregano, chopped
- ⅓ cup Greek olives (or green olives if you prefer), chopped

Pound chicken until about ½ inch thick.

Dredge chicken with flour and seasoning.

Heat oil in large pan. Add chicken and brown on each side, about 4 minutes.

Transfer chicken to a plate and keep warm.

To pan with chicken juice, add leek and garlic. Cook about 1 minute.

Add wine and tomatoes and bring to a simmer.

Cook several minutes until slightly reduced.

Stir in herbs and olives.

Return chicken to pan.

Heat on low until heated through.

Serve on rice.

CHICKEN & SAUSAGE CASSOULET

Ingredients:
  ¾ pound dried navy beans or other white beans
  4 cups water
  2 cups chicken broth
  1 bay leaf
  1 teaspoon fresh winter savory
  ¼ pound country style or thick-sliced bacon, cut into small pieces
  6 chicken legs or 8 thighs or combination
  4-6 large carrots, cut into pieces
  2-3 onions, quartered
  1 pint canned tomatoes or tomato sauce
  ½ cup chopped celery and celery leaves
  3 large cloves garlic, diced
  1 teaspoon salt—or to taste
  2 teaspoons fresh sage, chopped
  ½ teaspoon fresh thyme
  ½ teaspoon black pepper
  ½ pound Andouillette sausage, cut into 1 inch pieces

Rinse beans. Place beans in large oven-proof kettle. Cover with water.
Bring to boil and boil 1-2 minutes. Cover and let sit 3-4 hours. Do
    not drain.
Add broth, bay leaf, and savory. Bring to simmer. Continue to simmer 1
    hour.
Meanwhile, in skillet, brown bacon until moderately crisp. Drain on
    paper towels, but allow drippings to remain in pan.
Brown chicken in drippings, adding a little butter if needed. Set aside.
Preheat oven to 350°.
Remove bay leaf from beans.
Add bacon, vegetables, tomatoes, salt, pepper, and herbs to the beans and
    broth. Top with chicken.
Cover and bake at 350° 1 hour. Uncover.
Add sausage and mix into top part of cassoulet.
Bake 30-45 minutes longer.

CHICKEN IN BASIL SAUCE

Ingredients:
> ¼ cup milk and 1 egg, whisked together
> ¼ cup corn flake crumbs or fine cracker crumbs
> 4 boneless chicken breasts
> Salt and pepper to taste
> 3 tablespoons butter, divided
> ½ cup red pepper, diced
> ¼ cup white wine
> ½ cup chicken broth
> 1 cup heavy cream
> ½ cup grated Parmigiano, Asiago, or Romano cheese
> ¼ cup fresh basil, chopped

Put milk/egg and crumbs in separate bowls.

Season chicken with salt and pepper, then dip it in milk, then in crumbs.

Heat 2 tablespoons butter in large skillet, then place chicken breasts in butter and cook about 5 minutes on each side until brown and cooked through.

Remove chicken and keep warm.

Add 1 tablespoon butter to skillet and heat.

Add red pepper to skillet and cook about 1 minute. Remove pepper to small bowl.

Add wine to skillet, stirring to release brown bits. Add broth. Bring to simmer.

Stir in cream. Add red pepper and heat until just bubbly.

Add cheese and basil. Stir, then add chicken and cook and stir until heated through.

Serve chicken with sauce poured over.

CHICKEN WITH HERBS, PEPPERS & OLIVES

Ingredients:
- 1 small to medium leek, thinly sliced (or substitute sweet onion)
- 2 large cloves garlic, minced
- ½ cup green pepper, chopped
- 1 jalapeno or other hot pepper, finely chopped
- 1 quart canned tomato sauce, or 5 large fresh tomatoes, chopped and lightly mashed.
- 1 teaspoon cumin, ground
- 1 teaspoon coriander, ground
- 1 tablespoon fresh oregano, chopped
- 1 cup Greek or black olives, sliced
- 2 tablespoons white wine vinegar or herb vinegar of your choice
- 8 chicken breasts or thighs or 2 whole chickens cut into pieces

Preheat oven to 350°.
Put all ingredients except chicken in sauce pan. Bring to boil.
Place chicken in shallow baking dish. Pour sauce over. Bake about 1½ hours or until juice in chicken runs clear.

CHICKEN WITH ROSEMARY SPRIGS

A quick, yet elegant, dish

Ingredients:
- 2 tablespoons olive oil
- 4 boneless chicken breasts
- Salt and pepper to taste
- 4 sprigs fresh rosemary
- ⅓ cup Italian herb vinegar or white wine vinegar

Heat oil in large skillet.
Season chicken, then place in skillet and begin browning.
Put a rosemary sprig on top of each.
Sprinkle 1 tablespoon vinegar on chicken while browning first side.
Turn breasts over, putting sprig of rosemary on the side that has already been browned.
After browning 1 minute, reduce heat. Pour vinegar over chicken.
Cover and cook a few minutes until juices run clear.

CHICKEN WITH LEEKS & HERBS

Ingredients for marinade:
- ¼ cup balsamic vinegar
- 4 cups water
- ⅓ cup honey or sugar
- 1 tablespoon fresh sage, chopped
- 1 teaspoon fresh rosemary, chopped
- ½ teaspoon fresh thyme
- 1 clove garlic, in large chunks
- ⅓ cup coarse sea salt
- 1 cup hard apple cider
- 1 medium-large roasting chicken

Ingredients for finishing dish:
- 4 large leeks (or sweet onions)
- 1 cup chicken broth
- 2 tablespoons olive oil
- Salt and pepper to taste
- 1 tablespoon balsamic vinegar
- 1 tablespoon fresh sage, chopped
- 1 teaspoon fresh rosemary, chopped
- ½ teaspoon thyme
- 5 sprigs fresh rosemary
- ½ cup hard apple cider

Mix vinegar, herbs including garlic, water, sugar, and salt. Heat just to boiling. Cool. Add hard apple cider.

Place whole chicken in large bowl. Pour above mixture over. Place in refrigerator for several hours, turning chicken once.

Preheat oven to 375°.

Arrange leeks or onions on bottom of large baking dish.

Pour broth over onions.

Remove chicken from brine, dry with paper towels, put one rosemary sprig under skin over each breast, tie chicken up, and place over leeks.

Sprinkle chicken with olive oil, salt, pepper, vinegar, and herbs.

Lay 3 rosemary sprigs on top of chicken.

Roast chicken 2-3 hours or until 160°-170° internal temperature, basting during the last ½ hour with ½ cup hard apple cider.

CHICKEN WITH TARRAGON CREAM SAUCE

Ingredients for baking chicken:
  1 large whole chicken, cut into pieces
  3 tablespoons all-purpose flour
  Salt and pepper
  2-3 tablespoons tarragon vinegar (or white wine vinegar)

Ingredients for sauce:
  3 tablespoons all-purpose flour
  3 tablespoons butter
  ½ cup dry white wine
  1½ cups chicken broth
  2 tablespoons olive oil
  1 medium onion, diced
  1 teaspoon dry mustard
  1 tablespoon fresh tarragon, chopped
  1 teaspoon fresh thyme
  1 teaspoon salt (less if used canned chicken broth)
  Pepper to taste
  ½ cup sour cream
  Tarragon leaves or parsley to garnish

Preheat oven to 350°.
Add salt and pepper to flour. Dredge chicken pieces in flour.
Put chicken in baking dish and bake for 30 minutes.
Sprinkle with tarragon vinegar and continue to bake 25-40 minutes or until
    juices run clear.
While chicken is baking, melt butter in saucepan. Stir in flour.
Gradually stir in wine and broth. Simmer 5 minutes.
In another saucepan, sauté onion in olive oil until golden.
Add herbs, salt, and pepper and cook one minute.
Add onion-herb mixture to sauce and cook a few minutes.
Add sour cream and heat until bubbly.
Arrange chicken on serving plate; pour sauce over.
Garnish with tarragon leaves or parsley.

CHICKEN WITH CRANBERRY-ORANGE SAUCE

Ingredients:
 ¼ cup butter
 1 medium whole chicken, cut into pieces
 ½ cup freshly squeezed orange juice
 ½ cup cranberry juice
 ½ cup fresh cranberries (or ⅓ cup dried cranberries soaked in ⅓ cup
  cranberry juice for 1-2 hours)
 1 teaspoon fresh lemon thyme
 2 teaspoons fresh flat-leaved parsley, chopped
 1 teaspoon chervil, chopped
 Several leaves lovage, chopped (optional)
 5 leaves basil, chopped
 Salt and pepper to taste
 Parsley and/or orange slices to garnish

Preheat oven to 300°.
Heat butter in large pot. Brown chicken in butter.
Pour cranberry and orange juice over chicken. Add cranberries. Sprinkle
 with herbs, salt, and pepper.
Cover pot and cook in oven 2 hours, basting from time to time near the end.
Arrange chicken on serving plate, pour juice over it, and garnish with
 orange slices and/or parsley.

CURRIED CHICKEN

Ingredients for poaching chicken:
 Whole chicken, 4-5 pounds
 2 onions, quartered
 2 carrots, chopped
 1 rib celery, chopped
 1 bay leaf
 4 sprigs flat-leaved parsley
 3 sprigs lovage (or thyme—or some of both)
 1 tablespoon coarse sea salt
 10-12 peppercorns
 Water

Ingredients for curry sauce:
- 4 tablespoons shredded coconut
- 1 large onion, chopped
- 2 medium cloves garlic, minced
- ⅓ cup butter
- ½ teaspoon paprika
- 1½ tablespoons fresh ginger, grated or finely minced
- 1 teaspoon cinnamon
- ½ teaspoon cardamom, ground
- 1 teaspoon turmeric
- 1 teaspoon cumin, ground
- 1 tablespoon coriander, ground
- ¼ teaspoon hot pepper flakes or powder (more or less as you prefer hotness)
- 1 lime, juiced (or lemon)
- 2 tablespoons all-purpose flour
- ½ cup unflavored yogurt
- ½ cup sliced almonds, toasted
- 2 tablespoons cilantro or parsley, chopped

Put whole chicken, along with onions, carrots, and celery, in very large saucepan.

Add parsley, lovage, salt, and peppercorns.

Cover chicken with water. Poach about 2½ hours.

Lift out chicken, cool slightly, cut meat from bones and cut into small pieces.

Strain the liquid and add water or chicken stock, if necessary, to make about 4 cups.

For curry sauce:

Pour 1 cup of stock from poaching chicken over the coconut and let sit about 20 minutes.

Melt butter in large saucepan. Add onion and garlic and cook until golden.

Add herbs and spices and remaining stock. Simmer 15 minutes.

Add lime juice.

Strain coconut from juice. Add to sauce.

Stir flour into yogurt, then add to sauce, stirring well until slightly thickened.

Add chicken pieces to sauce. Reheat and add almonds and cilantro.

Let stand, covered, several minutes. Serve on couscous.

HERB-BRINED AND ROASTED CHICKEN

Ingredients for brining chicken:
- ⅓ cup coarse sea salt, dissolved in 1 cup hot water, then cooled
- 7 cups cold water
- 2 sprigs fresh rosemary
- 2 sprigs sage, thyme, or savory
- 2 cloves garlic, coarsely chopped
- Large roasting chicken

Ingredients for cooking brined chicken:
- 1 large clove garlic, coarsely chopped
- ¼ cup fresh rosemary, chopped
- 1 tablespoon other herbs of your choice such as sage, thyme, or savory
- 1 tablespoon fresh flat-leaved parsley
- 1 teaspoon coarse sea salt (or ½ tsp. table salt)
- 6-8 peppercorns (or ¼ teaspoon coarse black pepper) or more if you wish
- 2 tablespoons olive oil
- ½ cup dry red wine

Mix cooled salted water and cold water. Add herbs and garlic.

Place whole rinsed chicken in brine, after giblets are removed.

Place in refrigerator for 4-6 hours.

Preheat oven to 400°.

Using mortar and pestle, pound garlic, rosemary, choice of herbs, parsley, salt, and peppercorns together (or mix in coffee grinder or small blender).

Remove chicken from brine and pat dry.

Spread herb mixture over chicken, pushing some under skin.

Sprinkle olive oil over chicken.

Tie up chicken and place in roasting pan.

Roast chicken ½ hour.

Reduce heat to 350°. Add wine. Continue to roast, basting periodically until juices run clear and internal temperature in 160°-170°. Tent with foil, as necessary as chicken browns. (Entire roasting time will be about 2½ hours.)

LEMON CHICKEN WITH ROSEMARY SAUCE

Ingredients:
>   3 tablespoons olive oil
>   4 boneless chicken breasts or 6 boneless thighs
>   Salt and pepper to taste, going heavy on pepper
>   3 pounds small-medium new potatoes cut in half, (or left-over mashed
>   potatoes as described below)
>   2 cups chicken broth, divided
>   2 large cloves garlic, minced
>   ⅓ cup freshly squeezed lemon juice
>   2 teaspoons fresh rosemary, chopped
>   1 tablespoon fresh chives, snipped
>   1 tablespoon cornstarch mixed with a little
>   water
>   1 tablespoon butter
>   Lemon wedges for garnish, if desired

Heat olive oil in large sauté pan. Add seasoned
    chicken and brown on both sides.
Reduce heat and *add potatoes and 1 cup of stock. Cook gently for about
    15 minutes until potatoes are par-boiled and slightly soft.
While chicken is cooking, preheat oven to 350°.
Remove potatoes and chicken to ovenproof dish. Keep warm.
Return pan to heat. Add garlic. Cook about 1 minute. Add lemon juice and
    simmer 1-2 minutes.
Add second cup of chicken stock, rosemary, and chives.
Add cornstarch mixture. Bring to simmer and simmer 10 minutes to
    thicken and reduce slightly, then add butter.
Pour sauce over chicken and potatoes and heat in oven for 20-25 minutes.
Serve with lemon wedges as garnish, if desired.

*(If using left-over mashed potatoes, which may be substituted, don't
add potatoes with stock. Spread cold mashed potatoes in bottom
of ovenproof dish and heat 5-10 minutes in the oven until
warm. Add chicken and sauce and return
dish to oven for 20-25 minutes.)*

MARINATED TARRAGON CHICKEN BREASTS

Ingredients:
>   ⅓ cup lemon juice, preferably freshly squeezed
>   ⅓ cup orange juice
>   ⅓ cup tarragon vinegar (or white wine vinegar)
>   1 tablespoon fresh ginger, peeled and grated
>   ½ teaspoon ground coriander
>   2 cloves garlic, minced
>   1 tablespoon fresh tarragon, chopped
>   Salt and pepper to taste
>   2 tablespoons olive oil
>   6 chicken breasts—either bone-in or boneless
>   6 small sprigs fresh tarragon

In large bowl, mix all ingredients except chicken and tarragon sprigs.
Add chicken breasts and marinade in refrigerator at least 2 hours and not
    more than 6.
Remove chicken from marinade and boil left over marinade.
Heat olive oil on high in large skillet. Add chicken breasts and brown
    briefly on each side.
Put a sprig of tarragon on top of each breast. Pour reserved marinade over
    chicken breasts. Cook about 5 minutes, covered, or until chicken juices
    run clear.

RASPBERRY BALSAMIC CHICKEN WITH LEEKS

Ingredients for raspberry sauce:
>   ½ cup raspberry preserves (or fresh raspberries with honey added)
>   ¼ cup balsamic vinegar
>   ¼ teaspoon chipotle pepper, ground, or 1 teaspoon fresh jalapeno
>   pepper, finely minced
>   1 teaspoon fresh thyme
>   ½ teaspoon salt
>   Ground pepper as desired

Ingredients for cooking chicken:
>   4 boneless chicken breasts
>   Salt and pepper to taste

1-2 tablespoons olive oil
½ medium leek, thinly sliced, or ⅓ cup diced shallots
1 tablespoon raspberry vinegar (optional)
Sprigs of fresh thyme to garnish

Combine preserves and vinegar in small saucepan. Heat over medium heat
    until just bubbling. Add salt, pepper, and thyme. Remove from heat and
    set aside to use when chicken is browned.
Brown seasoned chicken in olive oil about 5 minutes, then flip and brown
    second side a couple of minutes.
Add leek or shallots and continue to brown another 5 minutes or until
    juice in chicken runs clear.
Add raspberry vinegar, if using, and heat 1 minute, then add raspberry
    sauce and heat a few minutes.
Serve with sprigs of fresh thyme as garnish.

MOROCCAN CHICKEN

Ingredients:
 1 tablespoon olive oil
 6-8 chicken thighs or legs
 2-3 carrots, sliced
 2 medium onions, sliced
 1 teaspoon salt
 1 teaspoon cinnamon
 1½ tablespoons fresh ginger, peeled and finely chopped or grated
 ½ teaspoon cumin
 1 small clove garlic, minced
 1 teaspoon fresh thyme
 1 teaspoon fresh oregano, chopped
 2 cups diced tomatoes
 ¼ cup honey
 ¼ cup green olives, sliced
 2 clementines, with each section chopped in half (or substitute raisins)
 Cilantro
 Prepared rice or couscous

Heat oil in skillet. Add chicken and cook until brown, turning once.
Leaving any stock in skillet, add carrots and cook until stock is gone,
    adding a little water if needed to par-cook carrots.
Add onions and continue to cook about 7 minutes.
Add salt, spices, and herbs.
Stir in tomatoes and honey.
Return chicken to skillet and simmer 5
    minutes.
Stir in olives and clementines and simmer
    10 minutes.
Taste and adjust salt.
Garnish with cilantro.
Serve with rice or couscous.

SPICY CHEESY CHICKEN WITH VEGETABLES

Ingredients:
  2 tablespoons olive oil, divided
  4 medium hot peppers or two hot peppers such as jalapeno or cayenne,
      finely chopped
  ¼ cup green pepper, chopped
  ¼ cup red pepper, chopped
  1 cup onion, chopped
  2 cups cooked chicken, chopped
  1 cup sweet corn kernels, fresh or frozen
  1 cup zucchini, chopped (optional)
  1 tablespoon cilantro, chopped
  ½ teaspoon cumin, ground
  ½ teaspoon paprika
  1 medium clove garlic, minced
  ½ teaspoon salt
  ¼ cup salsa
  1 cup cheddar cheese, shredded
  ½ cup crushed corn chips (or corn flake crumbs)
  Cilantro for garnish

Preheat oven to 350°.
Heat 1 tablespoon oil in small pan. Sauté peppers, then spread in 8-inch x
    8-inch or 9-inch round baking pan. Set aside.
Add second tablespoon olive oil to sauté pan. Put onion in pan and cook
    1-2 minutes until soft.
Spread out chicken on top of peppers.
Cover with onions and rest of ingredients through salsa.
Sprinkle with cheese, then crushed chips or crumbs.
Bake until bubbly—30-45 minutes.
Garnish with cilantro.

SPICY CHICKEN WITH PINEAPPLE SAUCE

Ingredients for herb/spice rubbed chicken:
 1 tablespoon brown sugar
 1 teaspoon medium coarse sea salt
 1 teaspoon coriander, ground
 ½ teaspoon black pepper
 1 teaspoon fresh thyme
 ½ teaspoon allspice, ground
 ½ teaspoon cinnamon
 ¼ teaspoon dried cayenne or other hot pepper, ground
 4-6 boneless chicken breasts or thighs
 2 tablespoons olive oil

Ingredients for pineapple sauce:
 1½ cups butter
 ⅓ cup packed brown sugar
 ⅓ cup dark rum
 1 cup canned crushed pineapple

Ingredients for completing dish:
 2 tablespoons olive oil
 2 medium cloves garlic, chopped
 1 leek or 4 green onions

Mix sugar, salt, and seasonings together to make a rub.
Drizzle the chicken with two tablespoons oil, covering both sides.
Sprinkle rub on each side of chicken, rubbing in well.
Refrigerate at least 1 hour.
While chicken is in refrigerator, combine butter, brown sugar, rum, and
    crushed pineapple in saucepan. Boil 10 minutes.
When chicken has been refrigerated at least 1 hour, heat olive oil in large
    skillet. Add garlic and leek/onions and cook until slightly soft.
Add chicken. Brown on medium heat 4-5 minutes each side.
Turn heat to low. Add pineapple sauce, scraping browned chicken
    residue into sauce; then flip chicken to first side.
Cook 2-4 minutes until chicken is cooked through.

Rice is a good accompaniment for this dish.

PORK

BRINED PORK ROAST WITH SAGE, ROSEMARY & THYME

Ingredients for brining pork:
>   7 cups water
>   ½ cup coarse sea salt
>   ½ leek, thinly sliced
>   2 large cloves garlic
>   Pepper to taste
>   1 bay leaf
>   Large sprig sage
>   Large sprig rosemary
>   Large sprig thyme
>   1 cup hard apple cider (or white wine)
>   1 pork loin roast, 3½-4½ pounds

Ingredients for roasting brined pork:
>   1 teaspoon herb-garlic rub (see page 101) or your favorite rub
>   2 tablespoons butter
>   2 tablespoons all-purpose flour
>   Rosemary or sage sprigs for garnish

Heat all brine ingredients except cider just to boiling. Cool, then add hard apple cider.

Pour brine over pork so pork is submerged. Refrigerate 6-24 hours. (The longer you brine, the more intense the flavor will be.)

Preheat oven to 375°.

Dry pork with paper towels. Rub with herb-garlic rub. Place in roasting pan.

Roast 15 minutes, then lower temperature to 300°.

Roast about 2 hours or until internal temperature of meat is 160°.

Let sit 5-10 minutes before carving.

In the meantime, make roux—melt butter, slowly add flour while mixing, then add juices from roast pork. Simmer until thickened.

Carve roast and serve with gravy.

Garnish serving plate with fresh rosemary or sage sprigs.

CROWN ROAST OF PORK

Ingredients:
- 1 tablespoon fresh lemon juice
- ¼ cup white wine
- 2 medium cloves garlic, minced
- 1 tablespoon fresh sage, chopped
- 1 sprig fresh rosemary, chopped
- 1 teaspoon fresh thyme
- 1 teaspoon fresh ginger, grated
- Salt and pepper
- 10-12 pound crown roast of pork
- 1 cup dried pears, coarsely chopped
- 1 cup dried apricots, coarsely chopped
- ½ cup apricot brandy or plain brandy
- 1 cup orange juice, divided
- 1 cup apple juice or hard cider
- 6 tablespoons butter
- 1 large onion, chopped
- 3 medium cloves garlic, minced
- ½ pound pork sausage
- 6 cups fresh bread crumbs
- Several sprigs fresh sage or thyme

Preheat oven to 350°.

Put lemon juice, wine, garlic, sage, rosemary, thyme, ginger, salt, and pepper in a bowl. Mix. Rub mixture over pork, reserving extra juice.

Place roast bone side down in large roasting pan, adding any juice left over from rub.

Roast about 3 hours, until internal temperature is 160°.

Meanwhile, put pears and apricots in large bowl. Add brandy and ½ cup orange juice. Allow fruits to soften at least 1 hour.

Melt butter in large skillet over low heat. Add onion and garlic and cook until soft, about 20 minutes.

Increase heat. Add sausage and fry about 10 minutes.

Transfer sausage and onion/garlic to bowl with fruit.

Add bread crumbs, remaining orange juice, and apple juice or hard cider.

Season with salt and pepper.

Put stuffing into baking dish and bake during last 35-40 minutes along with roast.

To serve, invert roast on platter, fill with stuffing. Garnish with sage or thyme.

PORK CHOPS WITH APPLES, THYME & LEEKS

Ingredients:
- 1 tablespoon olive oil
- 4 medium pork chops
- Salt and pepper to taste
- 1 medium leek (or sweet onion)
- 2 medium tart apples, such as Haralson, peeled and sliced
- ¼ cup apple cider, either sweet or hard
- 1 tablespoon cornstarch
- 1 cup chicken broth
- 2 teaspoons honey mustard
- 1 teaspoon fresh thyme

Heat oil in skillet on high.

Season chops with salt and pepper, then brown 2-3 minutes per side, depending upon thickness. Remove to plate.

Reduce heat to medium. Add leek or onion and brown until golden, about 2 minutes.

Add apples and apple cider. Cook about five minutes, until apples are soft.

Mix cornstarch with a couple tablespoons broth. When mixed well, add remaining broth.

Add broth mixture, mustard, and thyme to onion/apple mixture.

Bring to a simmer, stirring constantly.

Add pork chops; cook several minutes until pork chops are cooked through.

Garnish with fresh thyme sprigs.

PORK CHOPS WITH ORANGE SAUCE

Ingredients:
    2 tablespoons butter or olive oil
    4 pork chops, trimmed of excess fat, seasoned with salt and pepper
    1 cup orange juice, preferably freshly squeezed
    1 large clove garlic, minced
    1 teaspoon fresh thyme
    ½ teaspoon fresh sage, chopped
    1 teaspoon Worcestershire sauce

Heat oil or butter in large skillet. On medium heat, add pork chops and
    brown on each side about 4 minutes.
In meantime, combine orange juice, garlic, thyme, sage, and
    Worcestershire in a bowl.
Add orange juice mixture to skillet.
Reduce heat. Cook several minutes, turning chops over once, until sauce
    is reduced and chops are heated through.

PORK ROAST STUFFED WITH HERBS

Ingredients for brining:
    ½ cup medium coarse sea salt
    ¼ cup sugar
    6 cups water
    Boneless pork loin roast, about 3 pounds.

Ingredients for roasting:
    1 large slice dry bread, cut into small pieces
    ½ cup Parmigiano cheese, or your favorite hard and pungent cheese
    2 shallots (or 1 leek or sweet onion)
    ⅓ cup olive oil, reserving 1 tablespoon for browning meat
    ¼ cup basil, chopped
    1 tablespoon fresh thyme
    2 teaspoons fresh rosemary, chopped
    1 large clove garlic, minced
    ½ cup hard apple cider or dry white wine

Dissolve salt and sugar in 6 cups water. Cool.

In meantime, score fat on top of roast. Cut slit in side of roast, creating a
    pocket through the center, leaving ½-1 inch meat on three sides.
Submerge roast in brine and refrigerate 2 hours. Rinse and dry.
Preheat oven to 325°.
Using food processor, grind bread into crumbs. Put bread in a bowl. Mix
    with cheese, shallot, olive oil, basil, thyme, rosemary, and garlic.
Transfer to food processor and process until smooth.
Spread ½ herb mixture in pocket of roast. Tie roast with twine.
Heat remaining tablespoon olive oil in skillet. Brown roast quickly.
Remove roast to roasting pan. Spread remaining herb paste on top of roast.
Pour cider into skillet and scrape up brown bits; pour over roast
Roast at 325° until internal temperature of roast is 160°, 1-1½ hour.
Remove from oven and let rest 10 minutes before carving.

PORK TENDERLOIN IN TARRAGON SAUCE

Ingredients:
    2 tablespoons butter or olive oil
    2 medium leeks, thinly sliced (or substitute sweet onions)
    2 medium cloves garlic, minced
    ½ cup dry white wine
    1 cup chicken broth
    ½ cup sour cream
    2 tablespoons honey mustard or your favorite mustard
    2 tablespoons butter or olive oil
    2 pounds pork tenderloin, cut into 1-inch slices, seasoned with salt and
        pepper
    ¼ cup dry white wine
    1 tablespoon chopped fresh tarragon
    3 tablespoons fresh flat-leaved parsley, chopped
    Curly parsley for garnish

Heat butter or oil. Add sliced leeks and garlic and cook until golden.
Stir in wine, broth, cream, and mustard; then set aside.
Heat butter or oil in large skillet. Add tenderloin slices, brown well on each
    side, and cook until pork is done through, adding wine during last few
    minutes of cooking.
Add sauce, tarragon, and parsley to pork. Cook 2-3 minutes.
Transfer to serving plate and garnish with parsley.

ROAST PORK WITH HOT ORANGE SAUCE

Ingredients:

    Loin roast of pork, 4-5 pounds
    Salt and pepper, to taste
    1 teaspoon dried cayenne or hot chili pepper, ground
    1 tablespoon cumin, ground
    1 tablespoon coriander, ground
    1 teaspoon cinnamon
    1 cup orange juice, preferably freshly squeezed
    ½ cup white wine vinegar
    1 cup honey

Preheat oven to 350°.

Sprinkle pork with salt and pepper.

Place roast in oven and roast one hour.

While pork is roasting: Toast cayenne, cumin, coriander, and cinnamon 1-2 minutes over medium heat until spices smell toasted.

Mix orange juice, vinegar and honey in pan. Add spices. Bring to boil and simmer ½ hour.

Remove pork from oven. Pour sauce over. Roast about one more hour until pork is 160°, basting once or twice.

Let rest 10-15 minutes before carving.

ROSEMARY PORK CHOPS WITH ORANGE MUSTARD SAUCE

Ingredients:

    3 tablespoons olive oil
    4 thick-cut pork chops
    Salt and black pepper to taste
    1 teaspoon fresh rosemary, minced
    2 or more small sprigs fresh rosemary
    ⅓ cup white wine or hard apple cider
    ½ cup orange juice
    1 tablespoon honey mustard

Heat oil in skillet. Season chops with salt and pepper and rub in rosemary.

Place chops in pan and lay some sprigs of rosemary over.

Sauté chops 4-5 minutes per side, turning once and putting rosemary sprigs on top after turning to second side.

Add wine to pan juice and allow just to come to boiling.

Add orange juice and mustard.

Return to boil and heat on low-moderate until juice is reduced to about ½ and chops are cooked through, 8-10 minutes.

Serve with rosemary sprigs as garnish.

RIBS WITH ANISE, GINGER & ROSEMARY

Ingredients:
- 2 pounds pork country-style ribs, or spareribs if that is what you have available
- Pepper to taste and a very small amount salt
- 1 tablespoon olive oil
- 5 star anise, ground, or ¼ teaspoon powdered star anise
- 1 inch piece of ginger, peeled and grated
- 1 medium clove garlic, minced
- 1 teaspoon coriander, ground
- 2 bay leaves, ground
- Leaves from 2 sprigs fresh rosemary, chopped
- 1 cup rice wine
- ⅓ cup soy sauce
- ½ cup chicken stock
- ½ cup sliced leeks, shallots, or green onions
- ⅓ cup rice vinegar
- ⅓ cup brown sugar

Season ribs with salt, pepper, and star anise. Cut into serving-size pieces.

Heat oil in Dutch oven or other large pot over medium heat.

Brown ribs in oil—in 2 steps as needed.

Add spices, herbs, and wine. Heat to boiling

Add soy sauce, stock, and leeks, shallots, or onions. Simmer 20 minutes.

Add vinegar. Simmer about 1½ hours until meat is tender.

Stir in sugar. Simmer 15 minutes or more until sauce thickens slightly.

Serve with rice

FISH

BAKED WALLEYE FILLETS

  2 pounds walleye fillets
  ⅓ cup chopped green onion
  6-8 mushrooms, sliced
  ½ teaspoon salt
  ¼ teaspoon black pepper
  2 tablespoons dry white wine
  1 tablespoon fresh lemon juice
  ⅓ cup shredded cheese—your
      choice
  ½ cup fresh bread crumbs
  1 teaspoon fresh lemon thyme or thyme
  3 tablespoons flat-leaved parsley, chopped, divided
  2 tablespoons butter, melted

Butter a baking dish. Preheat oven to 400°.
Spread green onions and mushrooms over bottom of dish and place fish on
    top. Season with salt and pepper.
Sprinkle with wine, lemon juice, cheese, and bread crumbs; then sprinkle
    with thyme and 2 tablespoons parsley.
Drizzle with butter.
Bake 5 minutes; then loosely place foil over fillets.
Bake additional 7-10 minutes until fish is done.
Serve with fresh parsley sprinkled on fish.

FLOUNDER WITH GARLIC VINAIGRETTE

Ingredients:
  1-2 pound flounder (or other mild white fish), cleaned into fillets
  2 cloves garlic, finely minced
  1 tablespoon soy sauce
  3 tablespoons lemon juice

1 teaspoon honey
1 teaspoon fresh thyme
Salt and pepper to taste
¼ cup olive oil

Preheat oven to 450°.
After soaking and rinsing flounder, dry well.
Make vinaigrette by whisking remaining ingredients.
Place fish in baking pan and pour vinaigrette over, flipping fish over after
    adding vinaigrette. Refrigerate about 15 minutes.
Bake 8-10 minutes or until flesh is tender.

SALMON WITH CHIVE MUSTARD BUTTER

Ingredients for salmon fillets:
    2 tablespoons olive oil
    4 salmon fillets, skin removed
    Salt and pepper to taste

Preheat oven to 500°.
On top of stove, heat oven-proof skillet with oil.
Sprinkle salmon with salt and pepper.
Add salmon fillets to hot oil and brown on each side about 1 minute.
Place salmon in oven and bake 4-5 minutes or until tender.
Serve with chive mustard butter, below.

Ingredients for chive mustard butter:
    6 tablespoons butter at room temperature
    2 tablespoons lemon juice, ideally freshly squeezed
    2 teaspoons ginger, grated
    2 tablespoons fresh chives, snipped
    1 tablespoon honey mustard

Blend all ingredients. Spread on prepared fillets.

SALMON CAKES WITH DILL SAUCE

For cakes:
> 1 tablespoon olive oil, divided
> 1 small onion, finely chopped
> 1 stalk celery, finely diced
> 3 tablespoons fresh flat-leaved parsley, chopped
> 1 teaspoon fresh thyme
> 15-ounces canned salmon, drained, or 1½ cups cooked salmon
> 1½ teaspoons Dijon mustard
> 2 large eggs, lightly beaten, divided
> 1 tablespoon milk
> 1¾ cups fresh whole wheat breadcrumbs, seasoned with salt and
>   plenty of pepper

For creamy dill and parsley sauce:
> ⅓ cup mayonnaise
> ⅓ cup plain yogurt
> 2 scallions, finely chopped
> 1 tablespoon lime juice
> 1 tablespoon each fresh dill and flat-leaved parsley, finely chopped.

For garnish:
> Lemon wedges

Preheat oven to 425°.

Coat baking sheet with cooking spray.

Heat olive oil in nonstick skillet. Add onions and celery; cook, stirring, until softened, about 3 minutes. Stir in parsley and thyme. Remove from heat.

Place salmon in a bowl. Flake apart. Remove any bones or skin. Add mustard, ½ of the beaten eggs, and onion/celery mixture. Mix well. Shape into 6 patties.

Add milk to remaining beaten egg. Dip patties into egg mixture, then into breadcrumbs.

Heat remaining olive oil in skillet. Add 3 patties at a time and brown on low-medium heat until each side is golden, about 2 minutes per side.

Place cakes on baking sheet. Bake until heated through, about 15 minutes.

Meanwhile, prepare dill sauce by combining all ingredients.

Serve salmon cakes with dill sauce. Garnish with lemon wedges.

PASTA & RICE

CHICKEN LASAGNA

Makes plenty for a group or a large family

Ingredients :
    4 medium boneless chicken breasts
    Salt and pepper to taste
    2 tablespoons olive oil
    2 leeks, thinly sliced
    1 cup mushrooms, sliced
    2 large cloves garlic, minced
    1 tablespoon each fresh basil, thyme, rosemary, and oregano, chopped
    ½ teaspoon paprika
    ½ cup dry white wine
    ¾ cup chicken broth
    1 tablespoon lemon juice
    For white sauce: ¼ cup butter, ¼ cup all-purpose flour, and 2¼ cups milk
    1 pound mozzarella cheese, grated
    ¾ cup Asiago, Romano, or Parmigiano cheese, grated
    1 pound cooked lasagna noodles

Heat oil, then brown seasoned chicken breasts 4-5 minutes per side. Set aside.

Sauté leeks in pan juices, adding additional olive oil if necessary.

Add mushrooms and garlic. Cook until mushrooms are soft.

Stir in wine, broth, herbs, and lemon juice. Simmer 5-8 minutes.

Meanwhile, preheat oven to 350°.

Cut chicken breasts in half, then slice thinly and add to mushroom and herb sauce.

Prepare white sauce by melting butter, then adding flour and stirring until flour is dissolved. Add milk slowly and cook until thickened.

Using large baking dish, layer noodles, followed by chicken mushroom sauce, followed by mozzarella cheese, followed by white sauce. Repeat layers until ingredients are used.

On top, sprinkle Asiago, Romano or Parmigiano cheese.

Bake 45 minutes to one hour until bubbly.

GREEN BEAN WITH RICE CASSEROLE
(VEGETARIAN IF MADE WITH VEGETABLE BROTH)

Ingredients:
- 3 cups prepared, slightly undercooked rice (your favorite)
- 1 pound fresh green beans, steamed or boiled 3-4 minutes until slightly softened
- 2 tablespoons olive oil
- 1 medium onion, chopped
- 1 clove garlic, minced
- 1 pound fresh mushrooms (your favorite), cleaned and sliced
- 2 tablespoons butter
- 2 tablespoons all-purpose flour
- 1½ cups chicken or vegetable broth
- ½ cup dry sherry or white wine
- 1 tablespoon fresh herbs such as rosemary, thyme, basil, and/or oregano, finely chopped
- 1 teaspoon summer savory, chopped
- 1 tablespoon fresh flat-leaved parsley, finely chopped
- Salt and pepper to taste
- 1 cup half and half cream
- 1 cup shredded Parmigiano, Asiago, or your favorite pungent cheese

Preheat oven to 350°.

Put prepared rice in an ovenproof dish.

Heat oil in sauté pan. Add onion and garlic and cook two minutes. Add mushrooms and continue cooking 2 more minutes or until lightly browned. Set aside.

Melt butter. Add flour to make roux.

Slowly add broth to roux and cook until thickened. Add wine or sherry and simmer a few minutes.

Add herbs and salt and pepper to taste.

Add cream and heat briefly.

Mix about ⅔ of liquid with rice in the pan.

Mix remaining liquid with beans, onions, garlic, and mushrooms. Spread on top of rice.

Bake 20 minutes.

Add cheese and bake another 5 minutes.

MANICOTTI
(VEGETARIAN)

Ingredients:
- 12 manicotti shells, preferably whole wheat
- 3 cups shredded mozzarella cheese
- 2 cups ricotta cheese
- 2 cloves garlic, minced
- ⅓ cup fresh basil, chopped
- 2 tablespoons fresh oregano, chopped
- 1 quart jar homemade tomato sauce, or similar amount in cans
- 1 cup Parmigiano or Romano cheese, grated.

Cook pasta according to box directions or for 10-12 minutes. Drain and rinse with cool water.

While pasta is cooking, preheat oven to 350°.

Spray large baking dish with cooking spray.

Mix together the mozzarella, ricotta, basil, garlic, and oregano.

Stuff pasta shells with cheese mixture.

Pour ½ sauce into prepared dish.

Arrange pasta in dish.

Pour remaining sauce over pasta.

Sprinkle with cheese.

Cover with foil or other cover; bake 20 minutes.

Remove cover and bake another 20 minutes or until bubbly.

Recipes designated as **vegetarian**
exclude meat and fish. However,
a number of such recipes include cheese
and/or other milk products and therefore
technically are "lacto-vegetarian."

MINT COUSCOUS WITH ALMONDS & APRICOTS
(VEGETARIAN)

Ingredients:
- 2 tablespoons olive oil
- 2 shallots (or 4 green onions), diced
- 1 teaspoon coarse sea salt
- ½ teaspoon cinnamon
- 1 teaspoon coriander, ground
- 2 teaspoons cumin, ground
- ½ teaspoon turmeric
- 2 cups chicken broth
- ½ cup dried apricots, chopped
- 1¼ cups (uncooked) couscous, medium grain preferred
- ½ cup canned chickpeas (optional)
- ½ cup chopped fresh mint
- ½ cup toasted slivered almonds
- Lemon juice to sprinkle

Heat oil in saucepan. Add shallots or onions.
Add salt and spices and cook about 1 minute.
Add broth and bring to a boil.
Add apricots and remove from heat, letting the pot sit 5 minutes.
Return pot to heat and bring to a boil.
Add couscous and chickpeas, if using, and let sit off heat 7 minutes. Fluff.
Stir in mint and almonds and sprinkle with lemon juice.

ORZO STUFFED BELL PEPPERS
(VEGETARIAN IF USE VEGETABLE BROTH)

Ingredients:
    6 bell peppers of various colors with tops and seeds removed
    1½ cups orzo
    1 quart chicken or vegetable broth
    1 cup shredded carrots, steamed a few minutes
    3 cups fresh tomatoes, diced and mashed just a little to bring out juices
    1½ tablespoons fresh mint, chopped
    2 cloves garlic, minced
    Salt and pepper to taste
    ¼ cup olive oil
    ¾ cup Parmigiano or your favorite cheese, shredded

Bring large pot of water to boil. Put peppers in boiling water and boil 3-5
    minutes until just barely soft.
Preheat oven to 375°.
Cook orzo in broth.
Steam carrots 3-4 minutes.
Arrange slightly cooked peppers in baking pan.
Drain orzo and put in a bowl, reserving remaining broth.
Add tomatoes and steamed carrots to orzo.
Using mortar and pestle, mix together mint, garlic, salt, and pepper. Add to
    orzo, then mix in olive oil.
Spoon orzo mixture into peppers.
Place in oven and bake covered 45 minutes.
Remove dish. Sprinkle cheese over peppers and return uncovered to oven
    about 10 minutes until cheese is melted and slightly browned.

PARSLEY AND LEEK PESTO FETTUCCINE
(VEGETARIAN)

Ingredients:
    1 pound fresh green beans, trimmed and cut in half
    1 pound uncooked whole wheat fettuccine or your favorite pasta
    3-4 Italian tomatoes, thinly sliced
    1 cup parsley leek pesto (see page 106)

1 tablespoon lemon juice
Medium coarse sea salt and pepper to taste
½ cup Parmigiano, Asiago, or Romano cheese, freshly grated

Put a large pot on to boil with about 1 gallon water.
Steam green beans over separate pan with boiling water until tender, 5-6
    minutes. Set aside.
While beans are steaming, put fettuccine into boiling water. Boil 10
    minutes. Drain. Transfer to large serving bowl or plate.
Add green beans, pesto, sliced tomatoes, lemon juice, salt, and pepper.
Toss and sprinkle with cheese.

PASTA WITH GARBANZO BEANS & OLIVES
(VEGETARIAN IF USE VEGETABLE BROTH)

Ingredients:
    12 ounces of your favorite pasta (penne, elbow, or spirals work well)
    ¼ cup olive oil
    1 red onion, chopped
    ¼ teaspoon hot pepper flakes (or hot pepper sauce)
    4 medium cloves garlic, minced
    7.5-ounce jar artichoke hearts, packed in water or marinated (your
        preference), drained and chopped
    1 yellow or red pepper, chopped
    2 large tomatoes, chopped, or 1 cup tomato sauce
    1 cup vegetable or chicken broth
    2 teaspoons fresh basil, chopped
    15-ounce can garbanzo beans, drained
    1 cup olives (black, Greek, or green), sliced
    Salt and pepper to taste
    1 tablespoon flat-leaved parsley, chopped

Cook pasta according to directions.
While pasta is cooking, heat olive oil in skillet. Sauté onion until golden.
Add pepper flakes, garlic, artichokes, and pepper and sauté 1-2 minutes.
Add tomatoes, broth, basil, olives, beans, and seasoning. Simmer 5 minutes.
Drain pasta, pour sauce over and sprinkle with parsley.

PEPPER FETTUCCINE
(VEGETARIAN)

Ingredients:
- 2 tablespoons olive oil
- 3 bell peppers, cut into strips
- 1 cup sliced onion, preferably red
- 2 large cloves garlic, minced
- 1 small hot pepper, such as cayenne, minced (use less if you don't like HOT)
- 6-ounce jar pitted Greek olives, sliced
- ¼ cup white wine vinegar
- ¼ cup balsamic vinegar
- Salt and pepper to taste
- 12-ounce package fettuccine, preferably whole wheat
- 2 fresh tomatoes, chopped
- ½ cup grated Parmigiano or Asiago cheese
- 2-3 tablespoons fresh basil, chopped
- ¼ cup flat-leaved parsley, chopped
- ¼ cup sliced almonds

Put large pot of water on to boil.

Heat oil in large skillet. Add bell peppers and onions. Stir frequently. Cook until onion is golden.

Add garlic, cayenne, olives, and vinegars. Cook several minutes.

Season with salt and pepper. Add tomatoes near end of cooking. Heat just until warm.

Meanwhile, cook fettuccine about 10 minutes.

Drain noodles and put in large bowl.

Add pepper/onion mixture, cheese, basil, and parsley. Toss.

Garnish with almonds.

TABBOULEH
(VEGETARIAN)

Ingredients:
- ½ cup bulgur wheat
- 3 tablespoons olive oil, divided
- 1 cup boiling water or vegetable broth
- 2 cups flat-leaved parsley, finely chopped
- ½ cup fresh mint, finely chopped
- ½ cup red onion, chopped
- 2 medium tomatoes, chopped
- 1 cup seedless cucumber, peeled and chopped
- 2 tablespoons lemon juice
- 2 tablespoons red wine vinegar
- ½ teaspoon cumin, ground
- Salt and pepper to taste

Stir together bulgur and 1 tablespoon olive oil.

Pour boiling water or broth over bulgur. Cover tightly and let stand 15-20 minutes or until bulgur is soft. Drain.

Transfer bulgur to serving bowl.

Add remaining ingredients and toss with remaining 2 tablespoons olive oil.

Refrigerate at least 2 hours to allow flavors to penetrate.

WILD RICE WITH CHICKEN AND DRIED FRUIT

Ingredients:
- 1½ cups wild rice, rinsed and uncooked
- 1 quart water (or broth, either vegetable or chicken—or combination of water and broth)
- 2½ cups cabbage, shredded
- ½ teaspoon salt
- 2 chicken breasts
- ½ cup dried cherries or apricots
- 2 tablespoons chives, finely snipped
- 2 tablespoons fresh mint leaves, minced
- ½ cup chopped nuts, such as almonds, hazelnuts, or walnuts
- ½ cup sour cream

Bring water to boil in medium pot. Add wild rice, cabbage and salt.
Cook rice 45 minutes to one hour, until rice just starts to puff and break open. Fluff.
In meantime, braise 2 chicken breasts until juices run clear. Cool slightly, then cube meat.
Add meat, cherries, mint, and nuts to rice and cabbage mixture.
Add sour cream. Toss and heat briefly on very low heat.

Salads

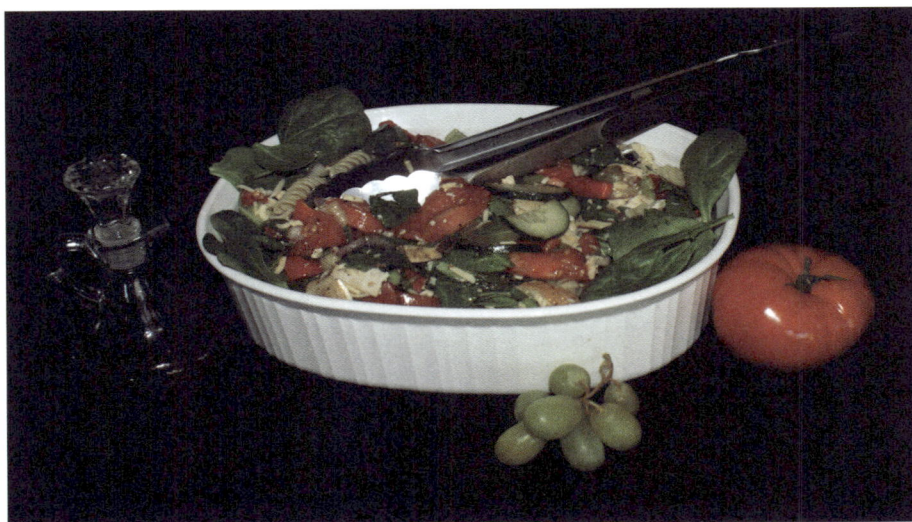

BEAN SALAD
(VEGETARIAN)

Ingredients:
    1 cup dried red kidney beans
    3 cups water
    1-2 tablespoons winter savory, chopped
    1 large clove garlic, minced
    1 teaspoon salt
    2 tablespoons olive oil
    1 tablespoon white wine vinegar
    ½ teaspoon lemon juice
    ½ cup celery, chopped
    ½ cup red onion, chopped
    ½ cup red bell pepper, chopped
    ½ teaspoon cumin, ground
    Salt and pepper to taste

Soak beans overnight. Drain.
Place beans in pot with 3 cups water. Add savory, garlic, and salt.
Cook until beans are soft, but still firm—1 to 1½ hour.
Drain and rinse in cool water.
Add remaining ingredients and blend.

BEET SALAD WITH MINT & FETA CHEESE
(VEGETARIAN)

Ingredients:
    6 beets, peeled
    ¼ cup balsamic vinegar
    2 tablespoons honey mustard
    ¼ teaspoon black pepper or to taste
    ¾ cup mint, chopped
    3 cups or so salad greens
    1 cup Feta cheese, crumbled
    Salt and pepper to taste
    1 tablespoon red wine vinegar
    1 tablespoon olive oil

Boil beets in water until soft, about ½ hour.

Drain beets, cut into slices.

Combine balsamic vinegar, mustard, and pepper. Pour over warm beets and marinade in refrigerator until cool.

While beets are cooling, mix mint, greens, salt and pepper, and cheese in a bowl.

Whisk together oil and red wine vinegar and pour over greens. Toss.

Put greens on serving plate and top with beets.

CELERY ROOT SALAD
(VEGETARIAN)

Ingredients:
- 1 cup mayonnaise
- 3 tablespoons Dijon or honey mustard
- 1 small shallot, finely minced
- 2-3 tablespoons freshly squeezed lemon juice
- 4 tablespoons flat-leaved parsley, chopped
- 1 teaspoon fresh rosemary, chopped well
- 2 teaspoons white wine vinegar
- 2 pounds celery root, peeled and chopped
- 1 large tart apple, peeled, cored, and chopped
- 2 teaspoons medium coarse sea salt
- Black pepper to taste

Combine mayonnaise, mustard, shallot, lemon juice, herbs, and vinegar in a bowl.

Add celery root and apple. Season with salt and pepper.

Cover and chill at least 1 hour.

CHICKEN PASTA SALAD

Ingredients for salad:
    4 chicken breasts, seasoned with the following:
        1 tablespoon fresh oregano, finely chopped
        1 large clove garlic, finely minced, or ½ teaspoon garlic powder
        Salt and pepper to taste
        1 tablespoon freshly squeezed lemon juice sprinkled on top
    1 pound dry pasta of your choice
    1 tablespoon olive oil
    1 large zucchini, sliced
    Sprinkle of garlic powder, oregano, and
        lemon juice
    2 cups fresh tomato, chopped
    1 red onion, chopped
    1 cup Greek or kalamata olives, sliced
    1 cup feta cheese, crumbled

Ingredients for dressing:
    2 tablespoons oregano, chopped
    1 clove garlic, finely minced or squeezed
        through a press
    ½ cup olive oil
    ¼ cup balsamic vinegar
    ½ cup mayonnaise
    1 tablespoon honey
    1 teaspoon honey mustard

Sauté seasoned chicken on top of stove or oven-bake until juices run clear. While chicken is cooking:
    Bring water to boil for pasta.
    Add pasta to boiling water and boil about 10 minutes or according to
        package directions.
    Heat olive oil in sauté pan. Add sliced zucchini and sprinkle with
        garlic. Sauté just a minute or so; then flip. Sprinkle with more
        garlic, a little oregano, and lemon juice.
    Prepare dressing by blending oregano, garlic, olive oil, vinegar,
        mayonnaise, honey, and mustard.
When pasta and chicken are done, slice chicken into pieces about ⅛ inch
    thick.

Combine tomato, onion, and olives. Mix with 2-3 tablespoons dressing.
Divide pasta between 4 plates.
Top with chicken, zucchini, and feta cheese.
Cover with tomato mixture.
Pour dressing over each plate, serving any extra for guests to add.

CHICKPEA SALAD
(VEGETARIAN)

Ingredients:
- ⅓ cup balsamic (or red wine) vinegar
- 3 tablespoons olive oil
- ½ teaspoon salt
- ¼ teaspoon pepper
- 3 medium cloves garlic, minced
- 2 15½-ounce cans chickpeas, drained (or 1 cup dried chickpeas, uncooked, then cooked)
- 1 cup red onion, diced
- 1 cucumber, sliced and halved
- 1 fresh tomato, diced
- ½ cup pitted kalamata olives or your choice of olives, halved
- 1 tablespoon fresh flat-leaved parsley, chopped
- 1 teaspoon fresh oregano, chopped
- 1 teaspoon fresh rosemary, chopped
- Fresh salad greens

Combine vinegar, olive oil, salt, pepper, and garlic in blender.
Combine chickpeas, onion, cucumber, tomatoes, olives, parsley, oregano, and rosemary.
Spread salad greens on individual plates or large serving plate.
Cover with chickpea mixture and serve with vinegar-oil dressing of your choice.

CORN AND BEAN SALAD
(VEGETARIAN)

Ingredients:
> 2 cups corn, cooked
> 1 can black beans, drained
> 1 clove garlic, minced
> 1 tomato, diced
> 2 small or 1 large medium hot chili
>   peppers, chopped
> ½ teaspoon cumin, ground
> 1 teaspoon fresh oregano, finely chopped
> 3 tablespoons olive oil
> 2 tablespoons red wine vinegar
> 1 tablespoon fresh epazote, finely chopped—if available
> Salt and pepper to taste
> Cilantro for garnish

Mix corn, beans, garlic, tomato, chili pepper(s), cumin, and oregano in
    small bowl.
Whisk together vinegar, epazote, salt, and pepper. Add olive oil to
    mixture and whisk or blend well.
Pour dressing over corn and bean mixture and blend slightly.
Garnish with cilantro.

CUCUMBERS IN CREAM
(VEGETARIAN)

Ingredients:
> 4 cucumbers, thinly sliced
> 1 cup sour cream
> 1 cup mayonnaise
> ½ cup sweet onion, chopped
> 2 teaspoons fresh dill leaves
> ¼ cup white wine vinegar
> 1 tablespoon honey
> Salt and pepper to taste

In a bowl, mix sour cream, mayonnaise, onion, dill, vinegar, honey and
seasoning. Whisk well. Add cucumber slices.
Refrigerate at least a few hours before serving.

FRUIT SALAD ON TENDER GREENS
(VEGETARIAN)

Ingredients for dressing:
- 1 medium clove garlic, pressed
- Leaves from a sprig each of fresh rosemary, chopped, and lemon thyme
- ¼ cup orange juice
- ¼ cup olive oil
- 2 tablespoons raspberry vinegar (or white wine vinegar)
- 2 teaspoons poppy seeds
- 1 tablespoon honey
- 1 green onion, chopped

Ingredients for rest of salad:
- 1 large orange, split into segments
- 1 cup dried cherries, cut in halves or quarters
- ½ cup dried apricots, cut into small pieces
- 1 cup celery, diced
- ½ cup red or orange bell pepper, chopped
- 1 pear, peeled and chopped
- 2 tart apples, peeled, cored, and chopped
- Lemon juice
- ½ cup pecans, toasted in a little butter and coarsely chopped
- Tender spring greens

Using mortar and pestle if available, mash together garlic and herbs for the
dressing; put in small blender along with other dressing ingredients,
and whisk until well blended.
Mix together fruits, pepper, and celery. Sprinkle with lemon juice.
Make a bed of greens. Top with fruit mixture. Sprinkle pecans over.
Sprinkle with a little dressing and put remaining dressing in server for
guests to add as desired.

GARDEN TOMATO SALAD WITH MEXICAN FLAIR
(VEGETARIAN)

Ingredients for the salad:
> 3 cobs fresh corn (or 1½ cups frozen)
> 1 large red onion, chopped
> 1 tablespoon butter
> 4 tomatoes, cut into chunks
> ½ cup canned black beans, drained and rinsed
> ⅔ cup cilantro, chopped, reserving some for garnish
> 2 avocados, peeled, pitted, and diced

Ingredients for the vinaigrette:
> 1 teaspoon cumin seeds
> 1 teaspoon medium coarse sea salt
> ¼ teaspoon hot pepper flakes
> Several black peppercorns
> ¼ cup fresh lime juice
> 1 clove garlic, minced
> ⅓ cup olive oil
> 1 tablespoon white wine vinegar, plus 1 teaspoon

Steam corn until just tender. Cut corn from cob.

Melt butter; then add onion and cook until tender. Mix corn and onion in small bowl. Cool slightly.

Add tomato, black beans, and ½ cup cilantro. Gently fold in avocado. Place in refrigerator until ready to serve.

Toast cumin seeds in dry pan, about ½ minute. Crush in mortar or spice grinder with salt, garlic, pepper flakes, and peppercorns.

Combine spices and lime juice. Whisk in olive oil and vinegar and blend well.

Drizzle salad with vinaigrette shortly before serving.

Sprinkle with salt and pepper to taste and garnish with chopped cilantro.

ITALIAN SALAD
(VEGETARIAN)

Ingredients for vinaigrette:
  1 cup olive oil
  ½ cup red wine vinegar
  1 large clove garlic, minced
  2 teaspoons fresh basil, chopped
  2 teaspoons fresh rosemary, chopped
  1 teaspoon fresh summer savory (if available)
  ½ teaspoon salt and plenty of pepper to taste

Ingredients for salad:
  1 head romaine lettuce—or your favorite greens
  1 cucumber, sliced
  1 cup feta cheese, crumbled
  1 cup green olives, halved
  1 red pepper, chopped and lightly sautéed in olive oil
  ½ cup sweet onion, sliced and separated into rings

Whisk together olive oil, vinegar, garlic, herbs, salt, and pepper.
In large bowl, combine lettuce and remaining ingredients.
Add about ½ of dressing and toss, reserving about ½ for guests to add, as
  desired.

PASTA SALAD WITH YOUR FAVORITE VEGGIES AND LEMON-HERB VINAIGRETTE
(VEGETARIAN)

Ingredients for salad:
- 1 pound of your favorite medium sized pasta (rotini, gemelli, and shells work nicely)
- 1 cup of your favorite cooked vegetables (asparagus, peas, green beans, corn), cooked until just tender-crisp
- 2 cups of your favorite raw vegetables (cucumbers, cut in half; cherry tomatoes, halved; carrots, cut into thin strips; snow peas, sliced; bell peppers, cut into strips)
- ½ cup canned artichoke hearts or chickpeas
- ¼ cup red onion, chopped
- 1 tablespoon flat-leaved parsley, chopped
- 1 tablespoon basil cut into thin strips
- ⅓ cup of your favorite olives (green, brown, or black), halved
- ½ cup feta cheese (or your favorite white cheese)
- 1 cup chopped fresh salad greens
- Freshly ground black pepper to taste

Ingredients for vinaigrette:
- ¼ cup fresh lemon juice
- 1 tablespoon honey mustard (or your favorite mustard)
- 1 tablespoon shallots, finely chopped (or leeks or green onions)
- 1 tablespoon honey
- 1 teaspoon lemon zest
- ½ cup olive oil
- 2 tablespoons fresh dill leaves, chopped
- 2 tablespoons chives, snipped
- 1 teaspoon fresh lemon thyme
- 1 teaspoon medium coarse sea salt
- ¼ teaspoon black pepper, freshly ground

Bring pot of water to boil and cook pasta according to directions.
Prepare cooked vegetables. Cool.
Chop and prepare fresh vegetables.
Prepare vinaigrette mixture.
Assemble salad by adding all ingredients, then toss with vinaigrette.

POTATO SALAD WITH FRESH HERBS
(VEGETARIAN)

Ingredients:
- 8 medium red potatoes
- ⅓ cup white wine vinegar, juice from dill pickles, or vegetable or Italian herbal vinegar
- 1 cup olive oil
- 1 tablespoon chives, snipped
- 1 teaspoon rosemary, chopped
- 1-2 teaspoons fresh dill leaves, chopped
- ½ teaspoon celery seeds
- ½ teaspoon fresh thyme
- Salt and pepper to taste
- 1 small red onion, diced
- ½ cup mayonnaise
- ½ cup sour cream
- 1 tablespoon Dijon-style mustard
- 4-5 boiled eggs, chopped
- ¼ cup fresh parsley, chopped

Cut potatoes in half and boil until tender but not mealy, about 15 minutes.
In meantime, whisk together vinegar, oil, herbs, salt, and pepper.
Drain cooked potatoes. Chop into bite-size pieces and put in a bowl. Add onion.
Put marinade/dressing over hot potatoes; cover bowl and let sit 20-30 minutes.
Stir in mayonnaise, sour cream, mustard, and eggs.
Chill for at least 2 hours before serving; then garnish with chopped fresh parsley.

RICE AND PINTO BEAN SALAD
(VEGETARIAN)

Ingredients for salad:
    1 cup long grain brown rice (ideally basmati)
    2 cups water
    15-ounce can pinto beans, drained (or cook your own)
    1 cup sweet onions or scallions, chopped
    1 bell pepper (your choice of color, but red or orange are nice)
    Cilantro, chopped, for garnish

Ingredients for vinaigrette:
    1 teaspoon cumin
    1 tablespoon fresh oregano, chopped
    1 teaspoon summer savory (optional)
    1 large clove garlic, finely minced or squeezed
    Salt and pepper to taste
    ¼ cup olive oil
    ¼ cup hot pepper vinegar (or use white wine vinegar and add scant ¼
        teaspoon hot pepper flakes)

Combine rice and water. Bring to a boil. Simmer 30–45 minutes until water
    is absorbed—or according to
    package directions. Cool.
In meantime, make vinaigrette:
    Toast cumin about 1 minute; then
        grind. Mix with oregano,
        savory, garlic, salt, and pepper,
        using a mortar and pestle if
        available.
    Put herb mixture, oil, and vinegar
        in a small blender and whisk
        until well blended.
Put rice in large bowl and mix in
    beans, onions, and pepper.
Pour dressing over and toss.
Garnish with cilantro.

ROASTED VEGETABLE SALAD WITH ROSEMARY VINAIGRETTE
(VEGETARIAN IF USE VEGETABLE BROTH)

Ingredients for salad:
  2 pounds small potatoes, quartered, preferably red
  1 pound green beans, ends trimmed
  1 red bell pepper, thinly sliced
  1 green pepper, thinly sliced
  1 red onion, sliced and separated into rings
  6 ounces chicken or vegetable broth
  1 medium clove garlic
  10-12 pitted kalamata olives, or your favorite olives, left whole to be
    added with dressing

Ingredients for vinaigrette:
  1 tablespoon olive oil
  2 teaspoons fresh rosemary, finely chopped
  1 medium clove garlic
  Black pepper to taste (use plenty)
  Salt to taste, if desired but not essential
  2 teaspoons lemon juice
  1 tablespoon red wine vinegar

Preheat oven to 425°.
Coat large baking dish with cooking spray. Spread potatoes, beans, peppers,
    and onion in dish.
Pour broth over with one clove garlic squeezed over top.
Roast ½ hour until vegetables are just tender, stirring twice during
    roasting.
In meantime, make the vinaigrette: Using mortar and pestle or small
    blender, blend oil, rosemary, garlic, salt, and pepper. Add vinegar and
    lemon juice and whisk well.
Put roasted vegetables in a bowl. Add dressing and olives. Toss.
Serve warm or chilled.

SHREDDED CHICKEN SALAD WITH HERB DRESSING

Ingredients for shredded chicken:
- 1 whole chicken
- 1 cup onion, sliced
- 2 ribs celery, left whole
- 1 teaspoon salt
- 10 peppercorns
- 2 sprigs fresh thyme
- 2 sprigs fresh tarragon
- 2 bay leaves
- 6-8 cups water

Ingredients for herb dressing:
- 3 tablespoons honey mustard
- 3 tablespoons tarragon vinegar (or white wine vinegar)
- 2 medium cloves garlic, minced
- ½ teaspoon salt
- ¼ teaspoon pepper
- Pinch or more cayenne pepper flakes
- ½ cup olive oil

Ingredients for finishing salad:
- 2-3 cups salad greens
- 12 or so cherry or grape tomatoes

Place chicken in a pot. Add next 8 ingredients, covering chicken with water.

Bring to boil and simmer gently about 45-55 minutes.

While chicken is cooking, make dressing by mixing ingredients in small blender, adding oil after you have started blending.

Remove chicken from pot and set aside to cool slightly.

Separate vegetables from broth. Discard veggies to compost. Keep broth in freezer or refrigerator for future use.

Cool chicken until you can pull meat from bones. Shred meat using 2 forks.

In a bowl, mix chicken and dressing, reserving a little dressing for drizzling on finished salad.

On individual plates or a serving plate, spread salad greens. Lay shredded chicken on top of greens and garnish with tomatoes.

SPINACH CHICKEN SALAD WITH HERB DRESSING

Makes plenty for a group

Ingredients for salad:
>   4 cups cooked chicken
>   2 cups green grapes, halved
>   2 cups torn spinach
>   1 red pepper, chopped
>   2 cups celery, chopped
>   8 ounces of your favorite pasta, cooked according to package
>   directions, drained and rinsed
>   1 cucumber, peeled and sliced
>   1 leek or small red onion, sliced or chopped
>   3 ounces dried apricots, chopped
>   1 7½-ounce jar marinated artichoke hearts, drained and chopped
>   ½ cup Asiago cheese, or your favorite
>   Orange slices and chopped parsley or celery leaves to garnish

Ingredients for dressing:
>   ½ cup olive oil
>   ¼ cup honey
>   2 tablespoons balsamic vinegar
>   1 teaspoon salt
>   1 teaspoon lemon juice
>   2 tablespoons fresh flat-leaved parsley
>   1 teaspoon fresh lemon thyme or rosemary, chopped
>   1 small clove garlic, pressed—or scant ¼
>   teaspoon garlic powder

Combine all ingredients for salad in large
>   bowl. Refrigerate while preparing dressing.

Combine dressing ingredients in small blender
>   and whisk—or whip well with wire whip.

Pour dressing over salad just before serving,
>   reserving some for individual additions,
>   as desired.

Garnish with orange slices and parsley or
>   celery leaves.

SPRING GREENS WITH TUNA & ROSEMARY-LEMON DRESSING

Ingredients:

    8 cups spring greens (lettuce, spinach, etc.), chopped
    ½ cup chopped red pepper
    2 ribs celery, diced
    ½ cup green olives, sliced
    12-ounce can tuna in water, drained

Ingredients for dressing:

    1 small fresh lemon, freshly squeezed (or ¼ cup bottled)
    1 tablespoon balsamic vinegar or soy sauce
    ¼ cup olive oil
    1 tablespoon honey
    Leaves from 1 sprig fresh rosemary, chopped
    Leaves from one sprig lemon thyme
    1 clove garlic, diced or squeezed (or ¼ teaspoon powder)
    Black pepper to taste

Combine greens, vegetables, olives, and tuna.
In small blender, blend lemon juice, vinegar, olive oil, honey, rosemary,
    lemon thyme, garlic, and pepper.
Pour dressing over greens and toss.

TOMATO & MOZZARELLA SALAD WITH HERBS (VEGETARIAN)

Ingredients for dressing:

    1 clove garlic, pressed or minced
    ½ teaspoon salt
    Black pepper to taste
    ¼ teaspoon (or less) hot pepper flakes
    1 tablespoon fresh oregano leaves, chopped
    1 tablespoon fresh lemon verbena leaves, chopped
    1 tablespoon fresh basil leaves, chopped
    1 cup olive oil

Ingredients for salad:

    5-6 fresh tomatoes, sliced
    1 pound fresh mozzarella, sliced into ¼ inch rounds.
    ¼ cup fresh basil leaves, finely chopped
    Lemon juice for sprinkle

For dressing, combine garlic, salt, pepper, pepper flakes, oregano, verbena, and basil. Blend in food processor. Gradually add olive oil while blending.

On platter, arrange tomato slices, alternating with cheese rounds.

Top with fresh basil.

Sprinkle with lemon juice; then drizzle with dressing.

WALDORF SALAD WITH INDIAN SEASONING
(VEGETARIAN)

Ingredients:

    ½ cup plain yogurt
    3 tablespoons mayonnaise
    ¼ teaspoon cinnamon
    1 tablespoon ginger, grated (or ¼ teaspoon ground ginger)
    Large pinch hot pepper flakes
    ¼ teaspoon cumin, ground
    ¼ teaspoon cardamom, ground
    ¼ teaspoon coriander, ground
    Large pinch turmeric
    ¼ teaspoon dry mustard
    Large pinch black pepper
    Large pinch salt
    1 orange, using 1-2 teaspoons of its zest, as well as orange sections
    3 tart apples, such as Haralson, chopped
    1 cup celery, chopped
    ½ cup golden raisins
    ½ cup walnut pieces, toasted

Whisk yogurt and mayonnaise. Add spices, pepper, and salt.

Grate zest from orange and add to above.

Separate orange segments. Add apples, celery, raisins, and walnuts.

Toss dressing with other ingredients.

SALAD DRESSINGS AND VINAIGRETTES

BALSAMIC VINEGAR & OIL DRESSING

Ingredients:
- ½ cup olive oil
- ¼ cup honey
- 2 tablespoons balsamic vinegar
- 1 teaspoon salt
- 1 teaspoon lemon juice, preferably freshly squeezed
- 1 tablespoon fresh parsley
- 1 teaspoon fresh thyme or lemon thyme
- 1 teaspoon fresh tarragon
- 1 clove garlic, minced

Put all ingredients in blender. Blend until smooth, blending again just before serving, if necessary

BASIL VINAIGRETTE

Ingredients:
- 3 tablespoons wine vinegar, red or white (or Italian herb vinegar)
- 2 tablespoons fresh lemon juice
- ⅔ cup olive oil
- ½ cup Parmigiano or Romano cheese, freshly grated
- 1 tablespoon fresh basil, chopped
- 1 teaspoon salt
- Black pepper to taste

Put all ingredients in blender. Blend until smooth.

BUTTERMILK RANCH-TYPE DRESSING

Ingredients:
- ½ cup buttermilk
- ½ cup mayonnaise
- 2 tablespoons white wine vinegar (or tarragon vinegar)
- ¼ teaspoon garlic powder or small clove garlic, minced
- ¼ teaspoon salt

½ cup chopped fresh herbs such as chives, tarragon, basil, or dill

Mix all ingredients in blender and blend until smooth.

CILANTRO DRESSING FOR SLAW OR OTHER SALADS

Ingredients:
- 1 cup sour cream
- ½ cup buttermilk
- ¼ cup white wine vinegar
- 2 teaspoons celery seed
- 1-2 tablespoons fresh cilantro, chopped
- 1 teaspoon salt
- 1 medium garlic, minced
- 2 tablespoons honey

Combine all ingredients in blender and blend until smooth.

DILL AND CHIVE VINAIGRETTE

Ingredients:
- ¼ cup fresh lemon juice
- 1 tablespoon white wine vinegar (or juice from dill pickles)
- 1 tablespoon prepared mustard of your choice
- 1 tablespoon shallot or green onion, finely chopped
- 2 teaspoons honey
- 1 teaspoon lemon zest, finely grated
- ½ cup olive oil
- 1 tablespoon fresh dill leaves, chopped
- 2 tablespoons fresh chives, chopped
- 1 teaspoon salt
- Pepper to taste

Combine lemon juice, vinegar, mustard, shallot, honey, and lemon zest.
Allow to sit to blend flavors for 10 minutes.
In blender, combine the above mixture with rest of ingredients and blend
until smooth.

FRESH HERB VINAIGRETTE

Ingredients:
⅓ cup white or red wine vinegar (or an herbal vinegar)
1 tablespoon fresh herbs such as basil, rosemary, thyme, or oregano—
    or a combination of herbs
¼ teaspoon dry mustard (or 1 teaspoon prepared mustard)
⅓ cup olive oil
Pepper to taste
1 tablespoon honey

Whisk well in small blender; as necessary whisk again just before serving.

GARLIC AND BASIL VINAIGRETTE

Ingredients:
½ cup olive oil
2 large cloves garlic, halved or quartered
¼ cup fresh basil leaves, pounded slightly but not chopped
¼ cup white wine vinegar (or Italian herbal vinegar)
1 teaspoon prepared mustard
½ teaspoon salt
Pepper to taste
2 leaves fresh basil, cut into small strips

Heat oil, then add garlic. Simmer 10 minutes on low. Remove from heat.
Add basil leaves to garlic oil. Let sit 20 minutes, then strain off garlic
    and basil, reserving oil.
Blend together vinegar, mustard, salt, and pepper, then slowly whisk in
    flavored oil until creamy.
Add basil strips to vinaigrette after blending. Stir.

MINT AND MELON DRESSING

Ingredients:
½ cup sour cream or vanilla yogurt
¼ cup mint-lemon balm white wine vinegar (or white wine vinegar)
2 tablespoons peppermint or spearmint, chopped
1 cup cantaloupe, chopped
Nasturtium flowers (optional)

Combine all ingredients, except nasturtium, in food processor and process
    until smooth.
Cover and refrigerate several hours before serving over cantaloupe cubes,
    strawberries, or your favorite fruit mixture.
Garnish with nasturtium flowers, if desired.

RASPBERRY VINAIGRETTE

Ingredients:
    ¼ cup white wine vinegar (or raspberry vinegar)
    1 teaspoon balsamic vinegar
    ¾ teaspoon fresh lemon thyme (or plain thyme)
    1 teaspoon prepared mustard
    ¼ teaspoon salt
    Black pepper to taste
    10-12 fresh red raspberries
    ½ cup olive oil
    1 tablespoon honey

Blend together the first 6 ingredients.
Add raspberries and whisk briefly.
Slowly add olive oil while blending. Add honey toward the end.

SOUPS

BARLEY VEGETABLE SOUP

Ingredients:
    ½ cup dry barley
    2 cups lamb or beef broth
    2 cups chicken broth
    2 large carrots, peeled and diced
    2 stalks celery, diced
    1 medium onion, coarsely chopped
    1 cup turnips or rutabaga, peeled and coarsely chopped
    1 large leek, sliced
    2 tablespoons flat-leaved parsley
    2 cloves garlic, minced or squeezed
    Salt and pepper to taste
    Parsley to garnish

Soak barley in water a few hours. Drain.
Combine all ingredients and simmer 2 hours or so.
Garnish with fresh flat-leaved or curly parsley, if desired

BEEF & WILD RICE SOUP WITH WINTER SQUASH

Ingredients:
    2 tablespoons olive oil
    1 pound beef chuck or round, cut into bite size chunks
    Salt and pepper to taste
    I large onion, diced
    2 cloves garlic, diced
    1 cup red wine
    8 cups chicken or turkey broth
    2 cups or so winter squash, peeled and cut into chunks
    1 cup wild rice, rinsed
    1 tomato, diced
    2 teaspoons fresh thyme
    1 teaspoon fresh sage, chopped
    1 teaspoon dried celery leaf (or one rib fresh celery, chopped)
    ½ cup fresh flat-leaved parsley, divided

Season meat with salt and pepper.

Heat oil in heavy sauce pan. Brown meat on all sides. Remove to a
   plate and refrigerate until rice mixture is done.
Reduce heat to medium.
Add onion and garlic and heat until onion is golden, scraping pan as needed.
Add wine and heat to boiling.
Add broth, squash, wild rice, tomato, herbs, celery leaf, and ⅓ cup parsley.
Reduce heat and simmer 1 hour or until wild rice is soft and grains have
   begun popping open.
Add beef and heat until beef is hot.
Add extra salt and pepper, if desired. Garnish with remaining parsley.

CARROT, CELERY ROOT & HOT PEPPER SOUP
(VEGETARIAN IF USE VEGETABLE BROTH)

Ingredients:
   1 tablespoon olive oil
   2 medium onions, chopped
   1 clove garlic, minced
   1 hot red pepper of whichever kind you prefer, diced
   3 medium celery roots, peeled and diced
   ½ pound carrots, peeled and chopped
   2 ribs celery, chopped
   6 cups broth—chicken or vegetable
   1 tablespoon cilantro, chopped, plus a little more for garnish
   Salt and pepper to taste

Heat oil in large saucepan.
Sauté onion until golden. Add garlic and red pepper. Continue to cook 1
   minute.
Add vegetables to saucepan and cook briefly, stirring.
Add broth and cilantro, reserving some for garnish.
Add salt and pepper to taste.
Bring to boil and simmer ½ hour.
With immersion blender or food processor, blend soup until smooth.
Warm up before serving
Garnish with cilantro.

CREAMY CARROT SOUP

Ingredients:
- 1 large onion, chopped
- 4 tablespoons olive oil or butter
- 1 pound carrots, scrubbed and cut in large pieces
- 1 teaspoon salt
- ½ teaspoon cinnamon
- 1-inch piece fresh ginger, peeled and cut into julienne strips (or ¼ tsp. ground ginger)
- 1 teaspoon fresh thyme (or lemon thyme)
- 5 cups chicken broth
- 1 cup heavy cream
- Sour cream or crème fraîche
- Parsley or chervil to garnish

Heat oil or butter in large saucepan.

Sauté onion in oil until soft and golden.

Add carrots and heat briefly.

Add broth, salt, spices, and thyme.

Heat to boiling and simmer 20 minutes or until carrots are soft.

Puree soup in 2 or 3 batches, blending until mostly pureed, leaving some small chunks.

Return to pot and heat until just bubbly.

Add cream and heat slightly, but not to boiling.

Top each serving with sour cream or crème fraîche and sprinkle with chopped parsley or chervil.

CREAM OF CILANTRO SOUP
(VEGETARIAN IF USE VEGETABLE BROTH)

Ingredients:
- 3 tablespoons butter
- 3 tablespoons all-purpose flour
- 1 large bunch cilantro (⅓-½ cup), chopped
- 1 quart chicken or vegetable broth
- 1 tablespoon olive oil or butter
- 1 large clove garlic, minced
- 1 medium sweet onion, chopped

¼ cup red bell pepper, chopped
8 ounces cream cheese
8 ounces sour cream
1 teaspoon cumin, ground
Salt and black pepper to taste

Melt butter and add flour to make roux.
Add broth slowly and cook until slightly thickened.
Process cilantro and 1 cup thickened broth in blender.
In sauté pan, put 1 tablespoon olive oil or butter. Add garlic, onion, and red
    pepper and heat about 3 minutes until slightly soft.
Put blended cilantro back in pot with remaining thickened broth. Add
    garlic, onion, and red pepper.
Add cream cheese and sour cream, stirring until well blended.
Add cumin, salt, and pepper.
Simmer 15 minutes, then adjust spices and serve.

CURRIED TURKEY SOUP

Ingredients for stock:
    Carcass of turkey, with most of meat carved off but a little left on
    10-12 cups water
    1 celery rib, 1 carrot, and 1 onion, all chopped

Ingredients for finishing soup:
    2 tablespoons olive oil
    1 medium onion, chopped
    2 ribs celery, chopped
    2 medium carrots, chopped
    1 teaspoon fresh thyme
    1-2 teaspoons curry powder (or your own mixture of some or all of
        the following: coriander, cumin, turmeric, cinnamon, cardamom,
        fenugreek, ginger powder, hot pepper flakes, paprika, and black
        pepper)
    2 tablespoons all-purpose flour
    1 large apple, peeled and chopped
    2 tablespoons honey
    1 pound small potatoes, scrubbed and quartered
    1 tablespoon parsley flakes
    Salt and pepper to taste
    1 cup unsweetened coconut milk or whole milk

After carving turkey, put in large pot with water, onion, celery, and
    carrot. Simmer very gently 1-2 hours. Remove carcass and bones. Cool
    slightly. Cut off turkey that is still on the bones and add to stock.
    (If desired, can refrigerate at this point and make the rest later.)
Heat oil in large skillet. Add chopped vegetables and cook just to
    soften, about 5 minutes.
Stir in thyme, curry powder, and flour and cook a few more minutes.
Add chopped apple, stir and cook just a minute.
Slowly add 1-2 cups stock to skillet and cook until slightly thickened.
Add honey and stir.
Put contents of skillet in stock pot. Stir.
Add potatoes, parsley, salt and pepper. Simmer ½ hour or so until potatoes
    are tender.
Remove from heat. Stir in milk and heat thoroughly.

DUMP AND POUR CHICKEN OR TURKEY SOUP WITH IMMUNITY BOOSTING HERBS

Especially good at the beginning of a cold or flu

Ingredients:

- Carcass of turkey or chicken, with a little of the meat left on
- Water
- Olive oil
- 1 large or 2 small onions, chopped
- 2 or more cloves garlic, minced
- Vegetables that you have on hand, such as carrots, celery, bell pepper, corn, etc., chopped if needed
- Shitake mushrooms—a couple ounces dried or 2-4 fresh
- Salt and pepper
- Herbs to your liking and taste, but especially including plenty of thyme and some turmeric and ginger. Other good additions are sage, rosemary, ground astragalus and/or goldenseal root or any herbs that have immunity-boosting properties
- 1-2 cups noodles such as Kluski egg noodles or any other you have, cooked
- 1-2 tablespoons balsamic vinegar or low sodium soy sauce to taste
- Salt and pepper to taste

After turkey or chicken has been carved, put carcass in large pot with plenty of water to nearly cover. Bring to gentle simmer (not a boil) for at least 1 hour until meat almost falls off carcass, then cool slightly. Trim meat off and return meat and broth to pot.

Heat olive oil in small skillet. Add onion and sauté until golden. Add garlic and cook another minute.

Add onion and garlic to pot.

Add mushrooms and vegetables such as carrots and celery to pot and simmer until soft.

Add any other vegetables you wish that need only a short time to cook.

Add herbs and noodles and continue to cook another 15 minutes or so.

Add vinegar or soy sauce, salt, and pepper

Enjoy and get well quickly.
Freeze the leftover soup for the next viral infection that comes along.

GARLIC POTATO SOUP
(VEGETARIAN IF USE VEGETABLE BROTH)

Ingredients:
- 2 tablespoons butter
- 1 large leek, thinly sliced
- 4 medium cloves garlic, pressed or finely minced
- 1 large garlic bulb with outer skins removed and the top ⅛ inch of bulb cut off
- 5 cups chicken or vegetable broth
- 2 bay leaves
- Salt and pepper
- 2 pounds potatoes, peeled and cut into small chunks
- ½ cup heavy cream
- 1 teaspoon fresh thyme
- 1 teaspoon fresh rosemary, chopped
- 3 tablespoons chives, finely snipped
- 1 cup shredded Asiago cheese or other cheese of your choice

Melt butter in heavy pan.

Add leek slices and cook until soft, but not brown.

Add minced or pressed garlic and cook about one minute.

Add broth, garlic bulb, bay leaves, and salt and pepper to taste.

Simmer 30-45 minutes, until garlic in bulb is soft.

Add potatoes and continue to simmer about 20 minutes.

Discard bay leaves. Remove garlic bulb and squeeze at bottom of bulb so that cloves slip out. Mash garlic.

Stir in cream, thyme, rosemary, and mashed garlic.

Blend in blender or use immersion blender, making soup creamy but leaving some small chunks.

If necessary, return soup to pot to heat. Stir in cheese.

Garnish with chives.

IRISH LEEK SOUP WITH SNAP PEAS & HERBS
(VEGETARIAN IF USE VEGETABLE BROTH)

Ingredients:
- 2 tablespoons butter
- 2 large leeks, thinly sliced
- 2 large cloves garlic, minced
- 1 pound new potatoes, scrubbed and diced
- 1 rib celery, diced
- 3 cups chicken or vegetable broth
- 1 cup sugar snap peas, stemmed and cut into ½ inch pieces
- 1 tablespoon fresh flat-leaved parsley, chopped
- 3 tablespoons fresh chives, snipped, reserving 1 tablespoon for garnish
- 1 tablespoon fresh dill leaves, chopped
- 1 teaspoon fresh chervil, chopped
- 3 cups milk
- 1 tablespoon fresh lemon juice
- ½ cup half and half
- Crème Fraîche (or sour cream) and snipped chives to garnish

Heat butter in large saucepan. Add leeks and cook until softened, about 4-5 minutes.

Add garlic and cook another minute.

Add potatoes, celery, and broth. Bring to simmer and cook until potatoes are just tender, about 15 minutes.

Increase heat. Add peas and cook until just tender, about 4 minutes.

Decrease heat. Add herbs and cook just a minute.

Remove from heat and let sit 10 minutes or until cool enough to put in blender.

Blend until smooth, adding some milk if needed.

Return to saucepan. Add milk and bring just to a simmer.

Add lemon juice, stir, then add cream.

Garnish with a dollop of crème fraîche and some snipped chives.

Serve immediately.

LENTIL SOUP WITH YOGURT

Ingredients for soup:
>   6 slices bacon, cut into small pieces
>   3 tablespoons olive oil
>   2 medium leeks, diced
>   6 medium carrots, diced
>   2 ribs celery, diced (or 1 rounded tablespoon dried celery leaf)
>   Coarse sea salt and pepper to taste
>   3 teaspoons cumin, ground
>   1 teaspoon coriander, ground
>   ½ teaspoon cinnamon
>   1-inch piece fresh ginger, cut into julienne strips
>   2 cups lentils, rinsed
>   6 cups water
>   ¼ cup fresh cilantro, chopped

Ingredients for garnish:
>   1 cup plain yogurt
>   2 tablespoons fresh mint, chopped
>   1 tablespoon fresh cilantro, chopped

Brown bacon in its own fat. Remove to plate.
Add oil to skillet. Add leeks, carrots, and celery.
Season with salt and pepper and continue cooking until vegetables are
>   slightly soft, about 10 minutes. Stir in spices and cook briefly.
Stir in lentils and water and bring to a simmer. Cover and cook until lentils
>   are tender, about 45 minutes.
Stir in cilantro and bacon.
If necessary, add more water and adjust seasonings.
In a bowl, mix yogurt with mint and cilantro
Serve soup with a spoonful of yogurt on top.

MINESTRONE

If desired, make a day ahead of time to let flavors develop

Ingredients:
>   ½ cup dried red beans (or 15-ounce can)
>   ½ cup dried white beans (or 15-ounce can cannellini beans)

6 slices bacon, cut into smaller pieces
1 large onion, diced
Olive oil, if needed
½ small green cabbage, sliced
3 medium carrots
3 ribs celery, chopped
1 medium potato
2 medium cloves garlic, diced
2 medium zucchini, sliced
2 10 ½-ounce cans beef broth or consommé (or homemade) or
    whatever kind of broth you have available
1 teaspoon coarse sea salt and pepper to taste
2 teaspoons fresh basil, chopped
1 teaspoon fresh thyme
1 teaspoon fresh oregano, chopped
1 teaspoon fresh winter savory
1 teaspoon fresh flat-leaved parsley
1 cup fresh green beans, cut in 1 inch pieces
½ cup pasta, uncooked (spirals, shells, or your favorite)
2 fresh tomatoes, chopped
½ cup fresh baby spinach leaves or other dark greens
Parmigiano cheese, grated

Soak beans in water overnight (unless you are using canned), keeping
    white beans separate from red.
Separately, cook beans with a little salt until just tender, about 45 minutes
    or more. Set aside, still keeping white and red beans separate.
Fry bacon in a pot or skillet until brown and crisp.
Remove bacon, leaving bacon fat in pot.
Sauté onion in bacon grease, adding olive oil as necessary.
When onion is golden, add cabbage, carrots, celery, potato, garlic, and
    zucchini. Continue to sauté until vegetables are slightly soft, about 20
    minutes.
Mash white beans and add to soup.
Add rest of ingredients except for red beans, spinach, and cheese. Simmer
    20 minutes.
Add red beans and spinach.
If desired, leave overnight in refrigerator and re-heat or serve immediately
    with Parmigiano cheese sprinkled on top.

PARSNIP SOUP WITH APPLES & SPICES
(VEGETARIAN IF USE VEGETABLE BROTH)

Ingredients:
    3 tablespoons butter
    1½ pounds apples, peeled, cored, and diced
    1½ cups parsnips, peeled and chopped
    1 small leek or sweet onion, chopped
    1½ teaspoon coriander, ground
    1 teaspoon cumin, ground
    1 teaspoon cardamom, ground
    1 large clove garlic, minced, or ¼ teaspoon garlic powder
    4 cups chicken or vegetable broth
    Salt and pepper to taste
    ⅓ cup heavy cream, or half and half if you prefer

Melt butter in large, heavy pan.
Add apples, parsnips, leek, spices, and garlic and heat through, allowing
    several minutes on medium heat.
Add broth and salt and pepper and simmer 1 hour or more.
Add cream just prior to serving.

VEGETABLES

APPLE CIDER SLOW-COOKED BEANS
(VEGETARIAN IF DON'T ADD HAM)

Ingredients:
- 3 cups dried beans—navy, great northern, cranberry, or your favorite beans for baking
- 750 ml. bottle hard apple cider (or sweet cider if you prefer)
- 1 large onion
- 1 apple, peeled and diced (or chopped dried apple, adding a little extra apple cider)
- ½ cup molasses (blackstrap is best)
- 1 tablespoon dry mustard
- 2 tablespoons tarragon vinegar, or white wine vinegar
- 1 tablespoon chopped tarragon leaves or chervil
- 1-2 inch segment fresh ginger, finely minced or grated (or ½ teaspoon ground ginger)
- 1 tablespoon coarse sea salt
- 1 cup diced ham or Canadian bacon (or sliced chopped bacon, slightly browned)

Sort beans. Rinse. Put in large bowl, cover with water by a few inches, and soak overnight.

Drain beans.

Put beans in large pot or Dutch oven. Add cider and bring to boil.

Reduce heat to simmer and simmer 30-45 minutes until beans are tender.

Transfer to slow cooker.

Add rest of ingredients and enough water to cover beans.

Cook on low about 8 hours, adding more liquid if necessary.

BRAISED CARROTS WITH MINT
(VEGETARIAN)

Ingredients:
- ½ cup sliced shallots or leeks
- 1 pound carrots, scrubbed well or peeled and cut in half lengthwise into 3-4" segments (or quartered if larger carrots)
- 2 tablespoons olive oil
- 1 tablespoon butter
- 3 cloves garlic, chopped
- 2 medium tomatoes, chopped
- ¼ cup fresh mint, preferably English mint or spearmint
- Juice from one small lemon, plus 1 teaspoon zest
- 2 tablespoons honey
- 1 teaspoon coarse sea salt
- ¼ teaspoon cumin, ground
- 1 teaspoon fresh chervil (optional)
- ¼ cup water, if needed
- Pepper to taste
- Curly or flat-leaved parsley, chervil, or mint, chopped, for garnish

Preheat oven to 350°.

Heat oil in Dutch oven or other ovenproof pot.

Sauté carrots several minutes until slightly browned. Add shallots/leeks and cook a few more minutes. Add garlic and cook about 1 minute.

Add tomatoes and rest of ingredients, except garnish.

Add water, if needed.

Cover pot and place in oven. Roast about ½ hour (or gently simmer on stove top).

Arrange carrots on platter and sprinkle with garnish.

CARAMELIZED ONIONS WITH PARSLEY, SAGE, ROSEMARY & THYME
(VEGETARIAN)

Ingredients:
> 5 large onions, sliced
> ¼ cup olive oil
> Salt and pepper
> ¾ cup balsamic vinegar
> 3 tablespoons honey
> 1 teaspoon each fresh thyme or lemon thyme, rosemary, sage, and
>   flat-leaved parsley, coarsely chopped

Slice onions.
Heat olive oil in large skillet.
Add onion slices and sauté until slightly brown.
Add salt and pepper.
Add balsamic vinegar.
Add honey and cook over low heat until the liquid begins to thicken.
Add herbs and continue to cook several minutes until liquid has a thin
caramel-like consistency.

EGGPLANT WITH TOMATO & HERBS
(VEGETARIAN)

Ingredients:
> 1 small eggplant
> 2 tablespoons olive oil or butter
> 1 small onion, sliced
> 1 clove garlic, minced
> 1 large or 2 small tomatoes, cut into chunks
> Salt and pepper to taste
> 2 teaspoons combination of fresh basil, rosemary, savory, and/or
>   oregano, chopped

Peel eggplant. Cut into 1-inch cubes.
Heat olive oil in skillet.
Sauté eggplant in olive oil until lightly browned.

Add onion and garlic. Sauté until onion is golden.
Add tomatoes.
Season with salt and pepper and herbs.
Cover and simmer for several minutes.

GARLIC GREEN BEANS WITH THYME
(VEGETARIAN IF USE VEGETABLE BROTH)

Ingredients:
> 2 slices bread, torn into small pieces
> 3 tablespoons butter, divided
> Salt and pepper to taste
> ¼ cup Parmigiano cheese, grated
> 2 large cloves garlic, minced or pressed
> 1 tablespoon all-purpose flour
> Large pinch hot pepper flakes or ground hot pepper
> 1 teaspoon fresh thyme
> 1 teaspoon fresh summer savory
> 1½ pounds fresh green beans
> ¾ cup chicken broth or vegetable broth
> 1 teaspoon balsamic vinegar

Heat ½ the butter in skillet. Add bread crumbs and cook until both are
    golden. Transfer to a bowl.
To bread crumbs, add salt, pepper, and cheese.
To skillet, add remaining butter. Add garlic and heat 2-3 minutes.
Stir in flour, pepper flakes, thyme, and savory.
Gradually add chicken broth, then vinegar, and bring to simmer.
Add beans and cook until beans are tender-crisp and sauce is slightly
    thickened, about 8 minutes.
Remove from heat.
Place in serving dish. Sprinkle with cheesy crumbs.

ROASTED POTATOES WITH HERBS
(VEGETARIAN)

Ingredients:
- 2 pounds potatoes, skins on, halved if small, and cut into chunks if medium or larger
- 1 tablespoon plus ⅓ cup olive oil (or melted butter)
- 1 large clove garlic, squeezed or ½ teaspoon garlic powder
- 2 tablespoons combination fresh chopped rosemary, thyme, savory, and oregano, going heavy on the rosemary
- Salt and pepper to taste
- 1 tablespoon freshly squeezed lemon juice
- 1 tablespoon fresh parsley, chopped and/or
- 1 tablespoon fresh chives, snipped
- 1 cup grated cheddar cheese, if desired

Soak cut-up potatoes in cold water 10 minutes.
Heat oven to 450°.
Drain potatoes and put on paper towels to dry slightly.
Use 1 tablespoon olive oil to coat bottom of large heavy baking sheet.
In a bowl, toss potatoes, ⅓ cup oil, herbs, garlic, salt, and pepper.
Spread potatoes on baking sheet.
Cover baking sheet with foil, folding foil over edges of pan.
Bake potatoes 10 minutes with foil on.
Remove foil, roast 20 minutes, then flip potatoes and continue to roast another 20 minutes.
Toss with lemon juice and fresh herbs.
If desired, cover with cheddar cheese and return to oven a few minutes until cheese melts.

SICILIAN PEPPERS
(VEGETARIAN)

Ingredients:
    ½ cup olive oil
    1 large red onion, thinly sliced
    2 large cloves garlic
    6 bell peppers—combination of green, yellow, red, or orange, as
        available, cup into strips
    1 cup tomato sauce
    1 small hot chili pepper, finely chopped, or ⅛-¼ teaspoon hot pepper
        flakes, depending upon your preference for heat
    ¼ cup capers
    1 tablespoon balsamic vinegar
    3 tablespoons basil pesto or 2 tablespoons fresh basil, chopped
    1 teaspoon fresh rosemary, chopped
    1 tablespoon flat-leaved parsley, chopped
    Black pepper to taste

Heat olive oil in large pot.
Add onions. Cook on medium heat
    about 5 minutes until soft but not
    browned.
Add garlic. Cook 1-2 minutes.
Add bell peppers, tomato sauce, chili
    pepper, capers, and vinegar. Stir.
Bring to simmer and simmer about 1
    hour.
Stir in herbs. Heat 1-2 minutes.
Add black pepper and serve.

VEGETABLE BAKE
(VEGETARIAN)

Ingredients:
>   2 medium onions, preferably combination of red and white, chopped
>   1 medium zucchini, sliced into ⅓-inch thick slices; then halved.
>   1½ cups fresh corn, just removed from cob—or frozen
>   2 sweet peppers, diced
>   4 medium tomatoes, diced
>   Juice of 1 small lemon
>   1 large clove garlic or 2 smaller ones
>   1 small chili pepper, diced
>   1 teaspoon fresh thyme or lemon thyme
>   ¼ cup salsa (from recipe page 110 or any salsa)
>   Salt and pepper to taste
>   1 cup grated Parmigiano, Romano, Asiago, or Monteray Jack cheese

Preheat oven to 350°.

Put chopped onion in a bowl.

Add zucchini to onions.

Slice kernels off cob and add to bowl.

Add peppers, tomatoes, lemon juice, garlic, chili pepper, thyme, salsa, salt and pepper. Mix.

Place everything in baking dish. Bake ½ hour.

Sprinkle with cheese and bake an additional 10 minutes or until cheese is melted.

WHITE BEANS WITH SAGE
(VEGETARIAN)

Ingredients:
>   1 pound dried cannellini beans or other white beans
>   6 cups cold water
>   ¼ cup olive oil
>   2 tablespoons fresh sage, chopped
>   1 large clove garlic, minced
>   ¼ cup onion, chopped
>   Salt and pepper to taste

Place dried beans in large saucepan and cover with water by a few inches. Soak overnight.

Drain beans and return to pan.

Add 6 cups water, oil, sage, garlic, and onion.

Bring to boil. Reduce heat to simmer. Cover partially and continue to simmer about 45 minutes until beans are tender.

Season with salt and pepper.

If desired, add a little olive oil on top for serving.

WINTER SQUASH WITH CIDER & HERBS
(VEGETARIAN)

Ingredients:
- 2 pounds winter squash, such as buttercup or delicata, cut into pieces about ½ inch thick
- 3 tablespoons butter
- ¼ cup fresh sage, chopped
- 1 tablespoon fresh rosemary, chopped
- 2 cups fresh apple cider
- 1 cup water
- 1 teaspoon salt
- Ground black pepper to taste
- 1 tablespoon white wine vinegar
- 1 tablespoon maple syrup

Melt butter in large skillet over low heat.

Add sage and rosemary. Cook 3 minutes.

Add squash to skillet and cook with butter and herbs for 1-2 minutes.

Add cider and simmer 20-30 minutes until squash is tender and cider has boiled down somewhat.

Add a little water if needed.

Season with salt and pepper.

Add vinegar and maple syrup. Cook additional 1-2 minutes.

MISCELLANEOUS INCLUDING APPETIZERS

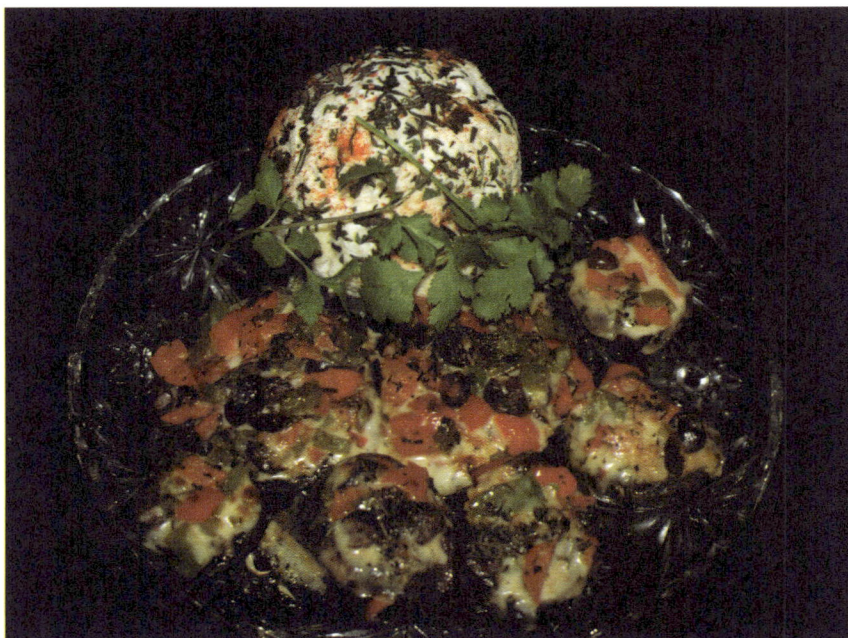

APRICOT PEAR SALSA

This salsa dresses up a simple chicken breast or pork chop

Ingredients:
- ¾ cup dry white wine
- ½ cup dried apricots, cut into quarters
- 2 firm pears, diced
- ½ teaspoon lemon zest
- 1 tablespoon lemon juice
- 1 teaspoon fresh rosemary, chopped
- ½ teaspoon fresh lemon thyme
- A sprig or two of fresh lemon thyme or rosemary to garnish

Combine wine and apricots in saucepan. Simmer about 10 minutes.

Remove apricots to a bowl, leaving juice in pan.

Add pears, lemon zest, and lemon juice to the wine and cook 5-7 minutes, adding herbs during the last minute or two (unless you use dried herbs, in which case they should be added at the same time as the pears).

Add pear mixture to apricots and toss.

Serve warm or cold.

CHICKEN OR TURKEY BROTH

Ingredients:
- Chicken or turkey carcass—after most of the meat has been carved off
- Water to cover carcass
- 1-2 tablespoons white wine vinegar, with or without herbs
- 1 small onion, diced
- Other vegetables, such as carrots and celery, diced (optional)
- 1-2 tablespoons herbs—your choice—either fresh or dried

Cover carcass with water. Add vinegar, onion, and any vegetables and herbs, and gently simmer 2-3 hours.

Remove carcass, cool slightly, and trim any meat left on carcass to use however you wish.

For broth, strain liquid into container.

Freeze for future use or refrigerate for use within a few days.

CORN BREAD STUFFING

Ingredients:
- 6 cups corn bread, broken into pieces
- 2 cups turkey or chicken stock
- 1 cup dried cherries or craisins
- 6 bacon slices, chopped
- 1 onion, chopped
- 1 celery rib, chopped
- Salt and pepper to taste
- 2 tablespoons fresh sage, chopped
- 2 tablespoons flat-leaved parsley, chopped
- 1 teaspoon fresh thyme
- ½ cup chopped nuts—hazelnuts, walnuts, or your choice
- 1 egg
- A sprig or two of fresh sage for garnish

Preheat oven to 350°.
Put corn bread on baking sheet and toast in oven 15 minutes.
In saucepan, heat stock. Add cherries or craisins.
Remove from heat and let sit while you complete remaining preparations.
In skillet, sauté cut-up bacon until slightly crisp.
Add onion and celery and cook about 5 minutes over medium heat.
Remove onions, putting in large bowl, leaving stock in pan.
Season onions with salt and pepper.
Add corn bread, bacon, nuts, and herbs to onion mixture.
Add egg to stock, whisking; then, add stock mixture to stuffing mixture.
Use mixture to stuff large turkey or put dressing mixture into a buttered baking dish and bake until browned, about 1 hour.
Garnish the dressing with a sprig or two of fresh sage.

CUCUMBER RAITA
(VEGETARIAN)

Excellent with hot Indian dishes, such as curries

Ingredients:
- 1½ cups plain yogurt
- 1 tablespoon lime juice
- 1 medium garlic, minced
- 1 cucumber, peeled, seeded, and chopped into small pieces
- ½ teaspoon cumin, ground
- 2 tablespoons fresh mint, finely chopped
- Salt and pepper to taste

Combine all ingredients.
Allow to sit in refrigerator for about ½ hour for best flavor development.

GREEN HERB DIP
(VEGETARIAN)

Ingredients:
- ½ cup green pepper, chopped
- ¼ cup sweet onion, chopped
- ¼ cup fresh parsley, chopped
- 1 cup tofu, crumbled
- 2 tablespoons olive oil
- 2 tablespoons lemon juice
- 1 tablespoon fresh dill leaves, finely chopped
- 1 teaspoon fresh lemon thyme
- Salt and pepper to taste

Puree green pepper, onion, and parsley.
Add crumbled tofu, oil, and lemon juice.
Blend in herbs, salt, and pepper.
Serve with celery or carrot sticks, broccoli florets, cucumber chips, or green or red pepper strips.

HERB BLENDS USING DRIED, CHOPPED HERBS

HERB-GARLIC RUB

2 tablespoons coarse sea salt
1 teaspoon peppercorns
1 teaspoon fennel seeds
1 tablespoon dried rosemary
1 tablespoon dried thyme
1 tablespoon dried oregano
1 tablespoon dried savory
1 tablespoon garlic powder (or less if you prefer a less garlicky rub)

Grind salt, peppercorns, and fennel, until salt is fine-medium, using
    mortar and pestle or small grinder.
Add other ingredients. Blend until leaves are chopped, but not powdery.
Store in tightly closed container.

ITALIAN BLEND

2 cups dried basil
1 cup dried oregano
1 cup dried rosemary
½ cup dried savory
1 tablespoon garlic powder *(I make powder from dried garlic cloves.)*

Blend in coffee grinder or other small blender just enough to break up
    herbs, but not so much you make a powder.

ENGLISH HERBS

1 cup dried tarragon
1 cup dried flat-leaved parsley
1 cup dried chives
1 cup dried rosemary
½ cup dried thyme
½ cup dried sage

Blend in same fashion as for Italian blend.

FINES HERBES

1½ cups dried tarragon
1½ cups dried flat-leaved parsley
1 cup dried chives
1 cup dried chervil

Blend in same fashion as for Italian blend.

HERBES DE PROVENCE

1 teaspoon dried rosemary
1 teaspoon fennel seed, slightly ground
1 teaspoon dried thyme
1 teaspoon dried savory
1 teaspoon dried basil
1 teaspoon dried tarragon
1 teaspoon dried dill weed
1 teaspoon dried lavender flowers
1 teaspoon dried oregano
1 teaspoon dried chervil

Blend in same fashion as for Italian blend.

HERBAL CHEESE BALL
(VEGETARIAN)

Ingredients:
  8 ounces goat cheese
  8 ounces cream cheese
  8 ounces Asiago or other pungent cheese, shredded
  ¼ pound cold butter
  1 medium clove garlic
  ½ teaspoon coarse sea salt
  ½ cup pecans, toasted and chopped
  2 tablespoons combination of rosemary, basil, thyme, oregano, parsley
      and chives, finely chopped and mixed together
  1 teaspoon orange zest
  ½ teaspoon dried paprika

Remove cheeses and butter from refrigerator and let stand at room
temperature ½ hour.
Using mortar and pestle, pound garlic and salt together.
On low speed, blend cheese, butter, and garlic-salt mixture in Vita-Mix,
blender, or by hand.
Add nuts and blend briefly.
Refrigerate ½ hour, then, using gloves, form cheese mixture into ball.
Mix herbs and zest.
Place cheese ball on serving plate; then sprinkle with herb-zest mixture and
paprika.
Refrigerate ball for at least 2 hours before serving.

HUMMAS WITH GARLIC & CUMIN
(VEGETARIAN)

Ingredients:
- ⅓ cup olive oil
- 2 large cloves garlic, thinly sliced
- 2 teaspoons cumin, ground
- 2 15½-ounce cans chickpeas, drained and rinsed (or 1 cup dried chickpeas, cooked)
- 3 tablespoons tahini
- 3 tablespoons fresh lemon juice
- 1 tablespoon soy sauce
- 1 teaspoon fine or medium sea salt
- ¼ cup water

Heat oil in small skillet.
Add garlic and cumin and gently cook about 3 minutes. Remove from heat.
Put chickpeas, tahini, lemon juice, soy sauce, and salt in a Vita-Mix or food
processor and blend briefly.
Slowly add oil with garlic and cumin while machine is running.
Add water and continue to process until creamy.

Keep in refrigerator, but best if served at room temperature.
Great with pita chips.

MINT SYRUP

Ingredients:
- 1 ounce fresh spearmint or peppermint leaves
- 1 cup sugar—superfine is best
- 1 cup water

Rinse mint and drain.

Put sugar in small blender and add mint. Pulse just to break up mint a bit—or crush sugar and mint together with mortar and pestle.

Put mixture in small saucepan.

Add 1 cup water and bring almost to simmer over medium heat, stirring until sugar dissolves.

As soon as sugar dissolves, remove from heat and allow to infuse for 20-30 minutes.

Strain, discarding mint.

Cool and store in refrigerator to use in alcoholic drinks (great with rum, a little lime juice, and club soda), on fresh fruit salad, in a smoothie, or added to tea.

MUSHROOMS STUFFED WITH WILD RICE & HERBS (VEGETARIAN)

Ingredients:
- 12-15 large mushrooms of your choice
- 2 tablespoons melted butter
- ½ cup wild rice, cooked
- 1 teaspoon fresh basil, chopped
- 1 teaspoon fresh thyme
- ½ teaspoon salt
- ¾ cup Romano, Parmigiano, or Asiago cheese

Prepare rice according to directions.

Preheat oven to 350°.

Cut the stem out of each mushroom, chopping and adding to rice.

Drizzle butter over mushrooms.

Mix cooked rice with herbs and salt.

Stuff mushrooms with the rice and herb mixture.
Sprinkle mushrooms with cheese.
Bake for 10-15 minutes. Serve warm.

OLIVE SALAD
(VEGETARIAN)

This is great on focaccia bread or to make muffaletta sandwiches

Ingredients:
>1 small red bell pepper, sautéed 3 minutes in a little olive oil
>1 cup green olives, drained and chopped
>1 cup pitted kalamata olives, drained and chopped
>2 tablespoons minced shallots or sweet onion
>¼ cup celery, finely chopped
>2 large cloves garlic, minced or pressed
>1 teaspoon each fresh basil, oregano, and rosemary, finely chopped
>⅔ cup olive oil
>1 tablespoon balsamic or white wine vinegar
>Black pepper to taste

Combine all ingredients and refrigerate at least 2 hours prior to serving.

For muffalettas, use a round or Italian
loaf of bread. Slice in half lengthwise;
then scoop out some of each
half of bread.
Drizzle with olive oil from the salad.
Place some olive salad in scooped-out
part of bottom slice.
Add your favorite sandwich meat and a
slice of your favorite cheese.
Add a little more olive salad on top,
then cover with top slice of bread.
Cut into serving pieces.

This salad also works as pizza topping, with tomato
sauce and cheese added if you wish.

PESTOS
(VEGETARIAN)

BASIL PESTO WITH PARSLEY

Ingredients:
- 3 cups moderately packed basil leaves
- ½ cup walnuts or pine nuts, toasted
- ¼ cup flat-leaved parsley
- 1 medium clove garlic, chopped
- Coarse sea salt and ground black pepper to taste (½ teaspoon salt and ⅛ teaspoon pepper works well)
- 1 cup grated Parmigiano or Romano cheese
- ½ cup olive oil

Put basil, nuts, parsley, garlic, salt, and pepper in food processor.
With food processor running, add cheese and slowly pour olive oil into the feed. Process until smooth, scraping as necessary.
Use fresh or freeze for later use.

(For an interesting and zesty taste, decrease basil by ½ cup. Add ½ cup fresh mint and a tablespoon or so freshly squeezed lemon juice.)

PARSLEY AND LEEK PESTO

Ingredients:
- 2 cups lightly packed flat-leaved parsley
- 1 cup walnuts, toasted and coarsely chopped
- ¾ cup Asiago or Parmigiano cheese, grated
- 1 cup thinly sliced leeks (or sweet onions)
- Salt and pepper to taste
- ½ cup olive oil
- 2 teaspoons lemon juice

Put parsley, nuts, cheese, leeks, and salt and pepper in food processor.
With machine running, slowly add olive oil; then add lemon juice and process until mixture is smooth.
Add 1-2 tablespoons water, if needed, if mixture seems too thick.

TARRAGON PESTO

Ingredients:
    1 cup well-packed fresh tarragon
    1 cup well-packed flat-leaved parsley
    ½ cup hazelnuts or sliced almonds, toasted
    ¼ cup olive oil
    1 tablespoon lemon juice
    1 tablespoon water
    1 teaspoon lemon zest
    1 large clove garlic, minced
    1 teaspoon salt
    Black pepper to taste
    A little more water, if needed, to thin

Add all ingredients to food processor.
Blend, stopping occasionally to scrape sides, until thick and smooth.
Add a little water if needed to thin.

RED PEPPER & OLIVES IN PORTABELLA CAPS
(VEGETARIAN)

Ingredients:
- 2 tablespoon olive oil
- 2 red bell peppers, chopped
- ½ cup Farmers cheese or other light cheese, shredded
- ½ cup Asiago cheese, grated
- ½ cup kalamata or other Greek olives, chopped
- 1 teaspoon garlic, minced
- 1 teaspoon fresh rosemary, chopped
- Pinch of red pepper flakes
- 1 tablespoon olive oil, divided
- 8-12 portabello mushroom caps, large or medium, with stems and gills removed
- 4 tablespoons lemon juice
- 1 tablespoon low sodium soy sauce

Preheat broiler.

Heat olive oil in skillet. Add chopped pepper and sauté 3-4 minutes, then put pepper in a bowl.

Add cheeses, olives, garlic, rosemary, and pepper flakes. Set aside.

To skillet in which peppers were sautéed, heat ½ tablespoon olive oil.

Put mushroom caps in oil and sauté about 2 minutes per side.

Mix ½ tablespoon olive oil, lemon juice, and soy sauce in small bowl. Brush mixture over stem side of mushroom caps.

Place mushrooms on broiler pan with stem side up and broil 2-3 minutes.

Fill mushroom caps with red pepper mixture.

Return to broiler. Broil on low until cheese is melted—about 3 minutes. Serve warm.

ROASTED GARLIC

A very basic recipe for roasting garlic for any purpose

Ingredients:
    Several or many bulbs of fresh garlic, unpeeled
    Olive oil

Heat oven to 350°.
Cut off tips of garlic bulbs about ⅛ inch so you can see tops of cloves.
Brush tops of cut-off bulbs with plenty of olive oil.
Set bulbs cut-side down on baking sheet.
Roast about ½ hour until garlic is soft when squeezed.
Cool slightly, then squeeze over small bowl. The cloves should slip out
    easily.
Mash for most uses.

SAGE AND THYME BUTTER SAUCE

Great on baked or crusted chicken, turkey, or pork

Ingredients:
    1 tablespoon butter
    1 medium shallot or ½ leek, minced
    ¼ cup dry white wine
    ¼ cup heavy cream
    ⅓ cup chicken broth
    3 tablespoons butter
    1 teaspoon fresh sage, finely minced
    ½ teaspoon fresh thyme
    Salt and pepper to taste

Melt butter in skillet. Add shallot and heat until soft, 2-3 minutes.
Add wine, cream, and broth.
Simmer very gently 8-10 minutes.
Whisk in butter slowly, stirring constantly.
Whisk in sage, thyme, salt, and pepper.
Serve warm.

SALSA
(VEGETARIAN)

Ingredients:
- 20 ripe tomatoes, finely chopped
- 24 assorted hot peppers, coarsely chopped
- 6 medium onions, finely chopped
- 12 tomatillos, finely chopped
- 4 medium cloves garlic, minced
- 4 tablespoons salt
- 1 cup white vinegar
- ¾ cup olive oil
- ½ cup each fresh basil, cilantro, and parsley leaves, chopped

Put tomatoes in large colander. Add chopped peppers, onion, tomatillos, and garlic.

Stir in salt and allow to sit and drain 2-3 hours.

After draining, stir; then transfer to large pot; add oil, vinegar, and herbs.

Cook over medium heat until bubbly.

Enjoy fresh or can according to general canning directions for salsa.

SPINACH DIP
(VEGETARIAN)

Ingredients:
- 8-10 ounces cooked spinach (fresh or frozen)
- ¼ cup sour cream
- 4 ounces cream cheese
- ½ cup mayonnaise
- ¼ cup sweet onions, green onions, or leeks, finely diced
- 1 tablespoon fresh dill leaves, chopped
- ¼ cup flat-leaved parsley, chopped
- 1 medium clove garlic, minced or pressed
- ½ teaspoon fresh lemon or plain thyme
- 1 large pinch hot pepper flakes (or about 1 teaspoon finely diced red chili pepper, depending upon how hot the pepper is)
- 1 teaspoon salt and black pepper to taste

1 large jar pimentos, drained, or 1 small red bell pepper that has been
   chopped and sautéed lightly in olive oil

Cook spinach until soft. Drain and cool (or, if frozen, thaw and squeeze out
   excess water).
Put all ingredients except pimento or red pepper in food processor and
   blend until smooth.
Put mixture in a bowl; cover and refrigerate unless ready to serve.
Just before serving, add pimento or red bell pepper.

STINGING NETTLE ARTICHOKE DIP
(VEGETARIAN)

Ingredients:
   2 14-ounce cans or jars artichoke hearts. (Use marinated artichokes if
      you prefer a pungent flavor or plain if you prefer more bland.)
   8 ounces cream cheese, softened
   1 cup tightly packed or frozen stinging nettle leaves, harvested in
      spring when plants are just 4"-6" high (or substitute spinach)
   1 cup mozzarella or Asiago cheese, shredded or grated
   1 cup sharp cheddar cheese, shredded
   ½ cup onion, diced
   1 large clove garlic, minced
   1 tablespoon combination of flat-leaved parsley, oregano, and
      rosemary, finely chopped
   ½ cup mayonnaise
   ¼ cup Dijon mustard
   1 teaspoon salt
   1 tomato, diced
   ½ cup Parmigiano, Romano, or Asiago cheese, grated

Heat oven to 350°.
Drain and chop artichokes.
Combine artichokes, cream cheese, stinging nettle, cheese, onion, garlic,
   herbs, mayo, mustard, and salt.
Put mixture into baking dish and bake 45-60 minutes until bubbly.
Remove from oven and top with tomato and cheese. Return to oven and
   bake until slightly brown on top (8-10 minutes).
Serve on bread chunks or crackers.

SUN-BREWED HERB ICED TEA

Ingredients:
    Mint leaves, red raspberry leaves, lemon balm,
        lemon verbena, and other herbs you have in
        your garden that sound good in a tea
    Cold water
    Mint syrup (see page 104)—1 tablespoon per
        cup or to taste
    Orange juice and a little lemon juice, if desired

Rinse herbs well and remove stem material.
Fill a gallon jar loosely with herbs.
Add water and put in sun to brew for at least several hours.
Strain off herbs and refrigerate tea.
When ready to drink, add mint syrup and, if desired, a little orange juice
    and lemon juice, along with some ice cubes.

TEXAS-STYLE SALSA WITH CUMIN FOR CANNING
(VEGETARIAN)

Ingredients:
    20 cups tomatoes (about ½ of a sauce variety), peeled and chopped
    5 cups green chilies (warm but not hot), seeded and chopped
    5 cups onions, chopped
    3 cups hot peppers such as jalapeno, serrano, or cayenne, seeded and
        chopped
    4 medium to large cloves garlic, minced
    1½ tablespoons salt
    1 tablespoon cumin, ground
    1 tablespoon fresh oregano leaves, chopped
    2 tablespoons fresh cilantro, chopped
    1 cup lemon juice
    ¾ cup white vinegar

Mix all ingredients. Heat together. Simmer 15 minutes.
Fill clean and hot pint canning jars.
Process in boiling water bath 20 minutes.